*baby you can*

**DR1VE MY CAR**

# baby you can
# DR1VE MY CAR

## KEITH BADGERY

JOHN BLAKE

Published by John Blake Publishing Ltd, 3 Bramber Court,
2 Bramber Road, London W14 9PB, England

First published in hardback in 2002

ISBN 1 904034 25 X

British Library Cataloguing-in-Publication Data: A catalogue record
for this book is available from the British Library.

Design by ENVY

Printed and bound in Great Britain by CPD (Wales)

1 3 5 7 9 10 8 6 4 2

Papers used by John Blake Publishing Ltd are natural, recyclable products made
from wood grown in sustainable forests. The manufacturing processes conform to
the environmental regulations of the country of origin.

Every attempt has been made to contact the relevant copyright-holders
but some were unobtainable. We would be grateful if the appropriate
people could contact us.

# Contents

# At Home with Mick and Jerry

## (and Sophie and Tim)

IT WAS THE CHRISTMAS before the millennium. I had been Mick Jagger's driver for many years now and was used to being called upon at any time of the day or night to collect Mick and deliver him to the most unlikely places at the drop of a hat. On this occasion I had left him at the fashionable Halcyon Hotel in west London; some hours later, there was a call to meet him by a side door. I drove to the pick-up spot and there was Mick in the company of a stunning blonde I'd never seen before. The couple got in to the car and I drove off to 192, the fashionable Notting Hill restaurant that featured in *Bridget Jones's Diary*. Thus it was that I first encountered the amazing model, Miss Sophie Dahl.

Sophie quickly got used to the problems involved in being Mick Jagger's girlfriend. I remember the events of one freezing cold morning in particular. Overhead the December sky was a forbidding grey, while frost crackled thickly on the ground. The wind whistled sharply through the trees and the few passers-by, who were risking the elements for a country walk, were wrapped up warmly in coats and scarves. It was arctic outside, the sort of day that made you want to stay in by a roaring fire with a nice warm cat and a nice warm whisky.

In the back of my car, though, enough heat was being generated to warm up Manhattan. Mick and Sophie Dahl had spent the night with the Dahl family in Great Missenden, once the home of the great children's writer Roald Dahl, who was Sophie's grandfather. Now the couple were giggling and cooing together as I drove them back to London. The house still belongs to the Dahl family and I'd driven Mick up the night before to see his new amour. His plans were unclear when we first arrived but by midnight it was obvious that all was going well: Mick stuck his head out of the door and told me I could go home. 'Pick me up at ten o'clock tomorrow,' he added, and then went back inside.

But in the roller-coaster world of Mick and Jerry, nothing is ever straightforward. In the ten hours between leaving Mick and collecting him the next morning, I'd had a call from Jerry's people. Jerry, who had been on safari with her new boyfriend, Tim Attias, in South Africa, was returning to London that morning. Could I pick her up from Gatwick at six o'clock? Yes I could, so I collected a sleepy but happy Hall and drove her to the home that the couple still share. There was just one problem. Mick didn't know she was back.

I was in a real dilemma. Not for the first time, I was caught up in the middle of a long-standing love triangle – or love quartet, rather – and I didn't know what to do. Should I tell Mick that his long-term love and the mother of four of his children was back in town? It seemed indelicate to say anything to Mick in front of Sophie, but neither did I want to parade Sophie under Jerry's nose. So without consulting anyone I stopped the car a little bit away from the house. Mick gave me a quizzical look. I gave him a look back that was intended to convey to Sophie this was prearranged and to Mick that the situation was problematic. He seemed to realise something was up, because he went off without another word.

Once Mick was out of sight, I restarted the car and drove in towards the centre of London to drop Sophie off. 'Does Mick know that Jerry's back?' I asked Sophie once we were underway.

Sophie's face fell. 'No, he doesn't,' she said. She looked out of the window and sighed. 'Bang goes my dinner,' she said.

\* \* \* \* \*

Mick Jagger and Jerry Hall live in an enormous house in Richmond, west London, which, like Dr Who's Tardis, looks modest on the outside and overwhelmingly large inside. And, as with everything in the world of Mick and Jerry, nothing is quite as it seems. Mick and Jerry's living arrangements are as unconventional as everything else in their relationship: the living space is actually made up of two big old Georgian semi-detached houses with two separate front doors. Jerry lives on the right-hand side and Mick lives on the left. Mick's half of the house is divided in to large apartments, out of which Mick owns only a couple, with the rest belonging to other people.

Mick's flat is on the ground floor and he also owns the top floor living space, which has been converted in to bedrooms to accommodate the children when they stay with him. Behind the houses there is a large garden, at the bottom of which are two cottages, both of them owned by Mick. Elizabeth, Mick and Jerry's seventeen-year old daughter, lives in one of them with her boyfriend, the South African model Damien van Zyl, with whom she previously shared a place in New York – a brownstone town house also owned by Mick but now sold. Elizabeth's relationship with Damien is quite as tempestuous as that of her mother and father: the couple have split several times but are currently, at least, happily living in sin.

Both parts of the Jaggers' house are decorated in a traditional style: bold-coloured walls and lots of paintings and antiques everywhere, covered in vases of flowers and bowls of pot pourri. The couple mix with real aristocracy as well as the rock version, something which is mirrored in the way they have decorated their home. Jerry's half of the house opens on to a big hall with a dining room immediately on the left. At the further end of the dining room there is another door, which divides the two halves of the house. Usually it's left unlocked, but when Mick and Jerry have had a row Jerry locks it until Mick comes crawling and gets her to start speaking to him again. She also locks the door when she's giving dinner parties or entertaining alone, which happens a lot more now than it used to.

Mick's flat is very elegant. The adjoining door leads in to his sitting room and study, which are separated by a large archway. The most obvious clue that the flat belongs to a rock star and not a viscount is a button on the wall which, when pushed, lowers a huge screen from the ceiling down in to the dividing arch. The screen can be used for films and television. Mick also has a music room, which is where the couple hold their joint parties; the room contains a piano and drum kit. Finally, there's a huge bedroom, complete with massive four poster, with an en suite bathroom. There's just one thing missing from the flat – a kitchen.

I discovered this one morning when I came round to collect Mick and found him looking thirsty and bad tempered at his front door. 'Look Keith, mate, can you go get me a coffee and a croissant?' he asked.

'Of course, Mick. Yvette run out, has she?' (Yvette is the household cook.)

Mick grunted and turned away. Later I was told that the problem was that Jerry had locked the adjoining door. Usually Mick would go through in to the main house for breakfast, but when he and Jerry had had a fight, the door would be locked and he would have two choices – to go all the way around to the other front door and let himself in, or to send someone else out to get his breakfast. Not wishing to concede any kind of defeat to Jerry (or to encounter a frosty welcome) that's usually what happens.

Jerry, on the other hand, does have a kitchen. Every day she wakes up at about 11 a.m. and Yvette makes her scrambled eggs with garlic and toast and strawberry jam. She is also partial to a cup of tea. Breakfast is a real event in the Jagger household: the table is laid the night before and piled high with cereals, home-made cakes and fresh orange juice.

The unusual living arrangement has suited the couple for a long time, not least because it means they have equal access to the children. But now that Elizabeth has moved away – even if it's only to the bottom of the garden – James is away at school during the week and the younger two are growing up, Jerry has finally decided that she really does want Mick to move away so that she can make a clean start, very possibly with Tim. So Mick and I have been looking at properties all over London.

At the time of writing, Mick has viewed between eighty and ninety houses but none, for whatever reason, has been up to his exacting standards. We even went to see John Cleese's house in Notting Hill, which is a fabulous place with a swimming pool – but only one bedroom. 'Where will the kids sleep when they come over?' Mick asked, and so that idea too was discarded. However, given the number of places that Mick's seen and turned down, he might well have an ulterior motive for wanting to stay put. He has tried to win Jerry back on numerous occasions and to this day his closest associates believe he still wants a reunion. And even if the couple never get back together, which is the most likely scenario now that Jerry has finally snapped, his continued presence means that Mick maintains at least some control over the situation. And Mick Jagger is very definitely a man who likes to be in control.

This came out very much during the making of the film *Enigma*, which Mick produced, and which was based on the Robert Harris novel of the same name. He was very much in command, often present during shooting.

Mick played a cameo role in the film, sitting in the officer's mess. To look the part, his long hair had to be kept out of sight under his hat, which meant that on one occasion I turned a corner and was rewarded with the unlikely sight of Mick Jagger wearing curlers. 'Why Mick, you're beautiful,' I announced.

'Leave it out, Keith, it's for the part. Glad my fans can't see me like this, though. Where's my hat?' After that, he kept his officer's hat on for the rest of the day – especially when Saffron Burrows, one of the film's stars, was around.

Much has been written about Mick's feelings about Kate Winslet, another of the film's stars, not turning up to the film's premiere and I can set the record straight about that right here: he was absolutely furious. Kate's marriage to film producer Jim Threapleton had just broken down and she issued a statement saying that due to personal pressures she wouldn't be attending the *Enigma* premiere. Mick put a good face on it in public, saying that after all, Kate had personal problems to face, but in private it was a different matter. When I came to collect him at the end of the evening, he got in the car with a face like thunder. 'That bitch,' he snapped.

'What happened, Mick?'

'Kate Winslet didn't show up.' He flipped open his mobile and for the rest of the drive back I could hear mutterings along the lines of 'absolutely disgusted', 'she should have made more of an effort' and 'she's a professional actress, isn't she?' Afterwards he laughed about it, but he saw absolutely nothing funny about Kate's absence at the time.

Producing *Enigma* gave Mick a taste for theatricals. When Jerry appeared as Mrs Robinson in *The Graduate* in the West End, he was extremely proud of her, but couldn't resist shoving his oar in. I collected the two of them from the theatre after he first went to see it – there was the usual crowd of two or three hundred that gathers wherever Mick is present, in this case milling around the stage door – and drove them on to the exclusive London eatery The Ivy. 'You were great, Jerry,' said Mick.

'Why thank you honey, I …'

'But you know that scene where you're walking around holding a glass? You should have a drink in that glass and a bottle in the other hand.'

'That's great advice honey, thank …'

'And you know that scene where you're sitting down most of the time? You should be standing up, walking around the stage.'

'That's a brilliant idea, Mick, and you know what …'

'Are you sure you're standing at the right angle?' Mick went on – and on and on. He was proud though, and not worried about the scene in which Jerry would have to appear naked – he felt it was done in good taste. He was only a little concerned about Gabriel, the Jagger's youngest child, going to see it.

Life with the Jaggers can be bizarre. One night I dropped Mick off at about three o'clock in the morning and just as I was driving off he rang me on my mobile. 'You've got to help me, Keith,' he said. 'I've got a bird in my room.'

'Lucky you,' I replied.

'No, it's a real bird. Come back and help me.'

I went back and there was indeed a finch fluttering around Mick's bedroom. We chased it for about an hour, trying to trap it with blankets and anything that came to hand, but it was hopeless – the ceilings in Mick's flat are very high and the wardrobes in his bedroom reach to within two feet of them, which provided an ideal nesting spot for the finch. Finally we left the poor little bird alone and got someone to trap it the next day. The Jaggers subsequently bought a second finch and the two birds now live in a huge cage in Jerry's kitchen, next to the goldfish. The family also has a variety of cats and dogs.

The Jaggers' kitchen is large and very well laid out, with a teak floor, teak wooden units and an Aga. Yvette the cook

17

has been with them for about fifteen years now and is originally from the Caribbean. Her specialities are fish, chicken, curries and cakes and the household's particular favourite – shepherd's pie. The family also has a couple of cleaners, one full time and one part time, two nannies and Quintin, their man in Mustique. Most of the year Quintin runs the Mustique home, but in the summer he comes over to England for a couple of months to act as the butler. Jerry also has a girl called Jane who comes in twice a week to help with paperwork and their accounts.

The pets can cause a problem. Yvette usually walks the dogs, but one day Mick decided to take Shadow, his jet black lurcher, out for a walk in Richmond Park. 'Come on boy!' he yelled as he left the house. 'Let's have some fun!'

They set off towards Richmond Park, Shadow trotting obediently at his master's side. 'Come on boy,' said Mick, absently getting out his mobile and keying in a number. 'Do you want to have a run, Shadow?' With that, he bent down and undid the lead. 'Hello?' he said in to his mobile as he did so. 'Hey baby, it's Mick …'

Now off the lead, Shadow had noticed something that Mick hadn't: a very large swan in the park's lake. Normally an obedient dog, Shadow lost control of himself and raced towards the lake, barking his head off. 'Yeah, babe,' Mick was saying, 'I can pick you up at …' The screams of onlookers alerted him to the fact that something was going on. Shadow had plunged in to the lake and was swimming out towards the swan. 'Call you back,' said Mick and clicked off his phone as he ran to the lake. 'Shadow!' he bellowed. 'Come back at once!'

Shadow took absolutely no notice: he'd got to the swan and sank his teeth in to her wing. The poor bird rose on her legs in the water and began to fight back, uncoiling her long neck and hissing and pecking at the dog. 'Shadow!' bellowed Mick. 'Get out of the water!'

By this time a crowd had begun to develop. 'That's Mick Jagger,' hissed one person.

'Nah, couldn't be,' said her companion.

'It is. Mick, it is you Mick, isn't it? Mick, can I have your autograph?'

Normally polite to his fans, Mick had no time to answer. He was getting increasingly desperate as Shadow and the swan fought on: shouting and bellowing was doing no good and he was on the verge of wading in to the water himself, when suddenly the swan whacked Shadow with her free wing. Shadow was so surprised – or hurt – that he let go and began making his way back to the bank as the crowd, which was by now quite considerable, watched his progress. 'Get back here, you rascal,' said Mick furiously, as Shadow scrambled on to the bank. 'You'll get me in trouble, you will, now get back on your lead you – oh, good evening officer.'

Someone had called the park police and now two of their number stood looking at Mick. 'Is that your dog, Mr Jagger – it is Mr Jagger, isn't it, sir?' asked the first one.

'Yes and yes,' said Mick sourly.

'Were you aware, sir, that every swan in England belongs to the Queen?'

'Blimey, is that right?' asked Mick.

'Yes, sir. And were you aware that you are not allowed to take your dog off the lead in the park?'

'No I wasn't, officer,' said Mick wearily. 'He's usually a good dog, I don't know what came over him –'

'No, sir,' interrupted the policeman. 'Now since this is your first offence – of this type, anyway –' the other policeman giggled – 'we'll say no more about it. But I must caution you, sir, that if you let this dog run amok like this again, we will be compelled to take action.'

'Yes, fine, thanks,' said Mick. At this point the park keeper arrived, with a vet in tow. 'That's the dog who did it!' shrieked one of the crowd, at which point Mick decided that Shadow had been out for quite long enough and that they were going back home. Yvette always walked the dogs after that.

\* \* \* \* \*

Mick and Jerry are still very affectionate with each other, though it is very unlikely they will ever get back together now. But the family continues to live what passes for a normal life in the Jagger-Hall household: they all use the big sitting room in Jerry's house and Gabriel, the youngest child, goes in to the smaller half of the house and wakes Mick up in the morning. Whatever his failings as a husband, Mick is a very good father and has become more so since the parting of the ways. He puts himself out more for the children, takes them out to shows and goes shopping with them.

In the documentary *Being Mick*, which was made by Mick's own film company Jagged Films, Mick confessed to an individual kind of morality, even if it's not the one recognised by most people. That might be the reason that Mick never brings women back to the flat, or almost never – there's a suspicion that Sophie's been there. Mick was serious about Sophie and they were together for a good year. But now he is back to seeing other women again.

No one can understand why Mick behaves as he does, although in the past Jerry has said that he wishes to go down in history as one of the world's great lovers. There are other factors at play: by virtue of actually being Mick Jagger, with the constant attention and the constant excitement at everything he does, his adrenaline levels are always extremely high. Mick also has a very high sex drive. Keith

Richards once told Mick he should go and see a doctor about it. Keith is the antithesis of his libidinous colleague and friend. Despite his heavy drinking, Keith is totally family oriented and when he's left on his own in England, he never messes around with other women.

The same can not be said for Mick. Before his relationship with Jerry finally and irrevocably broke down, there was a real chance that, even very late in the day, they might be able to repair the damage that had been done. The couple went out for a series of quiet dinners on their own and talked about what could be done. But even at that late stage, when Mick was quite genuinely trying his hardest to woo the most beautiful model of her generation back to his side, he could not bring himself to give up seeing other women.

Mick has got women everywhere, all over London and all over the world. There are some longer term liaisons and some very brief flings. He calmed down slightly when he was seeing Sophie but Mick Jagger without a harem of women is like salt without pepper, bacon without eggs. On one occasion we turned in to the driveway in Richmond and as we got out of the car, a girl appeared out of the shadows speaking in French. 'Leave it to me, Mick, I'll deal with this,' I told him.

'Nah, it's all right,' said Mick hastily and went towards the girl, also speaking in French.

I saw her pass him a slip of paper with her number on it. Mick called that number: it turned out that she lived in All Saints Road in Notting Hill Gate and wanted to meet up. And so they would 'meet' in her flat once a week: he'd get me to bring him a Chinese takeaway and then take him round to her place. This continued for months until Sophie came along, although he would be coy about admitting it. Once, when I collected him from the flat at about two in the morning, he said to me, 'I was watching a great film just now!'

'Yeah, Mick, of course you were,' I thought.

Then there's Vanessa Neumann in Lennox Gardens, the daughter of Mick's next-door neighbour in Mustique. This relationship has been widely publicised, as Mick has been photographed going in to her flat, and on one embarrassing occasion, the couple left the windows open, allowing the neighbours to hear them. Vanessa has been on the scene for some years now, at one stage seeing Mick once or twice a week, although Mick now sees rather less of her than he used to.

One of Mick's less well-known relationships was with the blonde, husky-voiced television presenter Mariella Frostrup in the summer of 2001. They had dinner on a number of occasions and Mariella went to stay at Mick's chateau in France – from which she returned on his private jet.

When Mick and Jerry split up, Mick had to go and stay at

The Dorchester. But Mick has long had a close relationship with a lot of London hotels. To accommodate all the girls, he keeps suites in various hotels for days at a time, mainly at Claridges and the Park Lane Hotel, and sometimes never even visits them. The arrangement would have all the complexity of a spy novel: someone would book the room under a false name, I would go and pick up the keys and hand them over. Mick would then make his way to the suite as unobtrusively as possible.

Sometimes, however, even Mick gets stood up or blown out and if that's the case he doesn't go to the suites at all. When Mick Jagger is stood up, he is not a happy man. He can be like a cat on a hot tin roof if he's in a partying mood. I've often known him to take out his phone at one o'clock in the morning and ring round to see if he can find anyone to visit. He sounds almost like a little boy: 'Come on baby, you know you want me,' he'll croon. Sometimes he's lucky and I drop him off somewhere for an hour, but sometimes he's not. 'Oh well, Keith, we'll have to go home,' he says and I take him back, a dissatisfied Rolling Stone.

\* \* \* \* \*

Mick is a very good mimic, and he particularly likes to put on silly war voices: 'I'm Biggs from the War Office.' He gets really carried away with his co-producer Matt Clifford, who's also one of his closest friends and both of them cluck away about passers-by – 'Ooh, look at that old dear over there doing her shopping. Ooh, I wonder what she's got in her bag. Ooh, and there's another old girl over there …'

Given the way that Mick treats his women, it would be easy to assume that he's really a misogynist underneath, but he's not. He genuinely prefers the company of women to men. Mick tries to be strict with his daughters, but it doesn't always work. He was angry when Jade, his daughter with Bianca, was expelled from school – like her father, she enjoys cavorting with members of the opposite sex – but he's much more relaxed about Elizabeth living with Damien.

Other than the womanising, though, Mick is actually a polite, gentlemanly figure. He is extremely business oriented: when he's in the car he's either constantly on his mobile or buried in the business pages of the newspaper. He's also very charismatic. When he walks down the street, people really do stop and stare at him and you can hear them saying, 'That's Mick Jagger!'

Sometimes he puts on a disguise – a silly hat, say – but that somehow just makes him look more like Mick than ever. He's never rude to anybody and he'll respond if people say hello, but he's perfected a technique of moving swiftly through the crowds when he doesn't want to be stopped.

And when he's doing business or visiting one of his girlfriends, he doesn't want to be stopped.

Jerry is much more fiery than Mick. When they have rows she usually manages to shout him down – not that Mick so much shouts as slightly raises his voice.

Jerry is a delight to be around, but she can come across as a bit of a diva, a Southern belle. She's lived in England so long now that she's acclimatised to this country, but you do still get a sense of the very poor background she came from. When she was a child living in Texas, the family didn't celebrate Christmas because they couldn't afford any presents. Jerry never even got a card. And on her birthdays, her mother would take her to the local store, point at the 'two dollar' shelf and say, 'You can have anything you want from there.' That would be Jerry's present for the year.

Even very poor Texans are courteous, though, and Jerry has incredibly good manners. On a daily basis she is nice, sweet and very thoughtful – she always sends flowers to friends who are ill – as well as polite. It's actually the children who rule the roost at home. James, the eldest, is away at Stowe during the week, but comes home at the weekend. Elizabeth is slightly scatty and always out and the younger two, Georgia May and Gabriel, are adorable little children.

Jerry also has a surprisingly down-to-earth side. She uses professional hairdressers when she wants to look particularly stunning, but otherwise she does her own hair herself, including dyeing it. Her hair can be a problem. Because it's so long it can look incredibly messy if it hasn't been properly groomed, at which point Jerry simply ties it up in a bun. She often gets in to the car with no make-up and applies it en route. Within ten minutes she goes from someone who looks if not exactly ordinary, then a pale version of Jerry Hall, to someone who is absolutely stunning. Jerry doesn't wear much make-up: mascara, foundation and pinkish blusher and lipstick. She has absolutely fantastic skin, which is almost translucent when you get close to her.

As you would expect, the children seem old for their years. Their conversation is more like that which you'd expect from an adult. Whenever Mick takes Georgia out in to London, she's always saying, 'Daddy, I'd rather go to Harrods and go shopping.' She's also a born comic and this quite frequently comes out when Jerry's been with Tim. In December 2001, Jerry went to Tim's house one Saturday and the next day I took Georgia and a friend out to meet them, as Jerry was buying Georgia a pony. When we got there, the girls hopped out of the car, stayed for half an hour and then raced back out again, accompanied by Jerry. Tim was coming along to help them pick the pony, but drove separately in his jeep so we could follow him. 'Please Mummy,' said Georgia firmly, as we set off, 'don't make me come here again. Tim's a hunter.'

'Don't be so rude,' said Jerry. 'Anyway, he's not a hunter, he's a polo player.'

'That's funny,' said Georgia. 'I saw a photograph of him in the house, and he was wearing a red jacket and everyone else was wearing black jackets. I suppose they're all polo players. Are they?'

'Don't be so rude,' Jerry repeated. Silence fell for a little while, which was broken when Jerry wound the window down to have a cigarette.

'Another one?' asked Georgia, pointedly. 'That's the second one you've had today. I suppose Tim makes you smoke more.'

The children are happy on the whole, though. Jerry is also extremely happy with Tim, who is a banker by day and a polo player in his spare time. He's a country man, totally different from Mick and Jerry met him through her previous boyfriend, the film producer George Saud. At 35 he's ten years younger than Jerry, but I would not be surprised if they got married – they behave like a couple of teenagers in love when they're together.

When Mick was away before Christmas 2001, Jerry held a dinner party for Tim's birthday at the Richmond house and she seems happier in herself than she has been for a long time. When the divorce was going through, she was quite seriously depressed that it had finally come to that – in fact, she was devastated. But now she's accepted it and wants to move on.

Jerry is happier to have her men in situ than Mick is with his women, although they are only invited when Mick's away. At the end of 1999 Mick took the children to Mustique, so Jerry promptly moved George in to stay for a couple of days and she also took him to Ronnie Woods's New Year's Eve party. She went off to Mustique a few days later, so George moved out again and the whole roller coaster went on.

Jerry eventually finished her relationship with George because she felt he was too young for her, but Tim is a different matter all together. Nowhere is this more evident than in the seemingly innocuous fact that Jerry's bought a mobile phone. This is significant because Jerry Hall hates mobile phones. She's convinced they spread dangerous levels of radiation and for years she used to moan about them – sometimes she wouldn't even let me use one to confirm her time of arrival for planes and so on. But at the end of 2001, Jerry actually went out and bought a mobile phone because Tim wanted her to. 'Tim doesn't realise what a big thing I've done,' she mused as I brought her back from the shops.

Jerry and Tim do little things that lovers do: they go

walking hand in hand in the rain together around his house in River, West Sussex, looking besotted with each other. When I collect Jerry, it's not unusual for Tim to say, 'Look after her, won't you.' And it might just be because of Tim that matters are finally coming to a head between Mick and Jerry. Mick's search for a new property has started again – and this time Jerry's getting involved in helping him find a new place, too …

# Wheels Within Wheels

THE 1980s was not a good decade for The Rolling Stones. The band had dominated the music scene for the best part of twenty years but increasingly it seemed the will was no longer there. Mick Jagger and Keith Richards began squabbling as they disagreed over the future direction of the band and Mick tried to carve out a solo career. As far as the music was concerned, Mick wanted a more contemporary feel while Keith wanted to stick to their rock roots: the result was the 1983 album *Undercover* – not one of their best – and *Dirty Work* in 1986, even less of an event. Mick did not help matters: he refused to tour in order to support the album and that lack of interest on his part was reflected on the part of the (non-)record-buying audience. For the first time since the band's formation it looked as if The Rolling Stones were nearing the end of the road.

This was to a great extent because Mick was concentrating on his solo career. He had always wanted to prove that he could make it alone as well as with the Stones and in 1985 he had a great success with the album *She's The Boss*. That was not to be easily repeated: his next effort, *Primitive Cool* in 1987, didn't even make the Top 40. Something in Keith seemed to snap, possibly caused by the fact that Mick refused to tour to support *Dirty Work*. Keith had always vowed he would never make a solo album, but changed his mind in 1988, with the release of *Talk Is Cheap*. The record contained a single entitled 'You Don't Move Me', a direct attack on Jagger. It seemed that it really was all over now.

Except that it wasn't. Reports of the demise of The Rolling Stones proved premature when the feuding songwriters packed up both their bags and their differences and went off to Barbados to work on a new album, *Steel Wheels*. This was supported by the 'Steel Wheels/Urban Jungle' tour, an extravaganza that proved the band had lost none of its musical brilliance or popular appeal. The Stones played 117 shows in sixty cities across three continents, selling 6.2 million tickets and grossing $140 million. The show was back on the road.

It was during the course of that tour that I met the band for the first time, although it would be some years before my relationship with Mick and Jerry really developed. I first heard The Rolling Stones when I was fifteen, back in 1964, but at the time it wasn't my kind of music. I was in to Rod Stewart, The Faces and The Who and didn't think much of the man with the strangulated voice. But a few years later, when I heard 'Honky Tonk Women' and 'Brown Sugar', I really began to get in to their music although I never dreamt I would one day meet them all.

So in 1989, when I was told I was going to be driving the Stones, I was really excited. I'd already driven some people who were big stars, such as Paul Young and Alison Moyet, but I'd never come across anyone in the same superstar league as the Stones. I was also very nervous. No matter how much you get used to rubbing shoulders with the rich and infamous, that slight attack of nerves never really goes away. In fact, on meeting the really famous, I still get a bit nervous to this day.

The first Stone I met was the mildest: Charlie Watts. I was sent to The Savoy to pick him up in a Daimler limousine – which he hated because he wanted something less ostentatious – to drive him to Cardiff to play Cardiff Arms Park with the rest if the band. Charlie looked older than I'd expected when he appeared, and he wasn't happy when he discovered each of the five Stones had a huge car to take them to Wales rather than travelling up all together. 'What a waste,' he muttered as we set off.

He put me at my ease immediately. Charlie is the best Stone to meet first, because he's utterly relaxed, utterly unpretentious and a very down-to-earth, nice man. 'Should I call you Charlie or Mr Watts?' I asked him as we set off.

He looked taken aback. 'What ever you like,' he replied.

I wasn't sure how to take this until a moment later Charlie announced, 'It's bloody big back here. Mind if I come and sit in the front with you?' And with that he clambered over the partition between the front and the back of the car as I was driving and spent the rest of the journey telling me about his watch collection and chatting about cricket. All of the Stones have a much wider range of interests than you would expect for people who are supposed to spend their entire time getting out of their heads. Even Keith is a surprisingly well-educated man.

Charlie wasn't happy, though, when he learned we were going to have a police escort in to Cardiff. The idea came from the police themselves, who were worried that the Stones would be mobbed if their cars broke down or got stuck in traffic and they weren't protected. The plan was that all five limos would meet at a prearranged point outside Cardiff and then would be escorted in to the town centre in style with sirens wailing, lights flashing and everyone getting a chance to show off. When we got there, though, we discovered that a couple of the other cars were an hour and a half away. Charlie was having none of it and demanded to be driven to the arena and so the police ended up giving us our own escort through the screaming crowds.

This protection, incidentally, is more important than just pandering to a pop star's ego. The terrible assassination of John Lennon remains a nagging nightmare to most major stars, for you never know whether there's a nut in the crowds who's decided that if he can't have you, no one else will. Even if the crowd is friendly, it can turn hysterical with potentially very nasty results – and that can happen fast. The most hysterical crowds I have ever seen were those surrounding Michael Jackson on the 'Dangerous' tour but the Stones, too, need protecting – even a mild-mannered Stone like Charlie Watts.

When massive stars do a gig, right afterwards they literally do a runner – straight from the stage to their waiting cars before the fans realise they've gone. So it was that night, and before the Stones had finished the gig, each car was packed with what the star would need on his way back to London. Every car had towels and a change of clothing – the Stones are drenched with sweat when they come off, but have no time for a shower – and any particulars the star requests for the journey back. The requests tend to reflect the individual's personality. Charlie had fruit, nuts and mineral water in his car; Keith had beer, vodka and scotch; Ronnie likewise; Mick had water and a specially made protein meal (Mick watches his figure like a hawk) and Bill had fruit, beers and wine.

It wasn't until we were well underway that Charlie realised his clean clothes had been stashed in the boot of the car rather than the back. I pulled away from the police escort, parked on the side of the M4, leaped out, gave him his change of clothing and continued on our way back to London as Charlie got changed in the back of the car. I had been introduced to The Rolling Stones and it was an association that was to last for very many years.

Charlie is by far the most laid back of the Rolling Stones. He genuinely doesn't know what all the fuss surrounding the band is about; he just does what he loves, which is making music. The adulation he and the rest of them get from the fans is a source of perplexity to the drummer: he, more than any of the others, remembers that there was a time when no one had heard of The Rolling Stones and that he, Mick and the rest of them were just a load of whey-faced schoolboys from South London. And the Stones seem to have become less important to him over the years. Back when I first met Charlie he was still a keen member of the group but these days his other interests are just as important: his brass band and the Halsdon Arabian stud he and his wife Shirley have near Dolton, north Devon, where they breed Arab stallions. The stables, which were built a few years ago, are more luxurious than most people's homes and they house up to one hundred horses, worth millions of pounds, at a time.

The couple are absolutely mad about animals, in the way that only the British can be. They have twenty-seven dogs, all of which live in the kitchen. Two were acquired as pedigree puppies as a gift from Sir Elton John, but many are rescue dogs from Battersea Dogs Home. Shirley, in particular, adores them. One on occasion in 1998, I drove her from Devon to Heathrow to catch the 10.30 a.m. Concorde. As soon as she landed in the United States, she was told that one of her dogs was seriously ill – so she turned right back and caught the next Concorde back to England. I received a call that she was on her way – 'Keith, you've got to help her,' I was told.

I collected a distraught Shirley from Heathrow and sped back to Devon. 'I knew the dog was ill but I had no idea how ill,' she said through her tears, and was too upset to say much more after that. The dog in question had been the first the couple had in Devon, the leader of the pack, and sadly had to be put down the next day.

Charlie's other great love is his brass band – a band that both Mick and Keith believe to be highly polished and professional. Both go along to support him, as does Ronnie, just as the others also go to support Ronnie's band. Because each of them does their own thing away from the Stones, they can be very supportive of each other without the internal rivalries and jealousies that caused so much trouble between Mick, Keith and Brian Jones in the early days of the band.

Charlie and Shirley – who is a sculptor in her own right, by the way – have a long-term, happy marriage. Of all the Stones it is Charlie who seems the most normal: very happy with his wife, his daughter Serafina, and his life. He and Shirley don't go out much and they don't make a fuss about anything – many's the time that I've taken Shirley to go shopping at the local Europa when they're in London in their house in Chelsea's Cheyne Walk. They are a very homely couple.

The next Stone I drove, about a year later, was Ronnie Wood, whom I had the task of taking to Wembley. He conforms much more closely to the stereotype of a Stone with a taste for the wild life. I collected him and drove off. 'Keith mate,' he said almost as soon as we started, 'you wanna pull up, yeah?'

'Why Ronnie, what's wrong?'

'There's no booze in the back of the car,' said Ronnie, sounding outraged, and so we stopped at an off licence almost immediately to fill the car up with beers – a not-untypical occurrence with Ronnie and Keith. No matter what the time of day or night, Ronnie always has a pint of Guinness in his hand, which could get him in to trouble with Jo, his wife. On one occasion, I was called out to collect Ronnie from Keith's house in Wimbledon, the idea being that I would take him to see his mother after stopping off at his own house. It didn't quite work out that way. Ronnie had been on an absolute bender all night with Keith, a fact that did not go unnoticed by Jo, who objects when Ronnie's drinking gets too out of hand. They went upstairs to have a row while I stayed behind in the kitchen: 'Where do you think you're going!' yelled Jo as soon as they were out of sight.

'I'm going to see my mum!'

'Oh no you're not, you're going to bed!'

'I tell you, I'm going to see my mum!'

'GO TO BED!'

There was a long silence. A few minutes later Ronnie came back downstairs, looking sheepish. 'I've changed my mind, Keith,' he announced aggressively, not quite catching my eye. 'I've decided I'm not going to Mum's after all.'

And then there was Keith. I first met Keith in 1992, when

he came to London from his home in Connecticut for a series of meetings in London. He staggered off the plane wearing exactly the kind of clothes he wears on stage, blinking slightly like a vampire who's been exposed to the sun and waving two walking sticks about, which he calls his 'rain sticks'. Like the Native Americans, Keith has decided that when he waves them around, the rain clouds will gather over his head and start a downpour. A long history of failing to produce so much as a trickle of water has done nothing to discourage him. The sticks, incidentally, are beautiful: bespoke, with ivory handles. 'All right, mate!' he roared at the top of his voice. 'I'm Keith!'

Keith might have given up the drugs, but he still has a drink and behaves as a rock and roll star should: he's totally alive. I call him Trevor and he calls me Kevin; unlike Mick, he's extremely chatty and friendly and usually sat in the front of the car to talk. Keith is just as flamboyant as you'd expect and always out of it: once while I was waiting for him in the kitchen in the late morning, he staggered in, fresh out of bed, lurched over to what he thought was the fridge and grabbed a bottle of vodka. It was actually the freezer and the vodka in the bottle was frozen. Keith upended it over a glass and a look of incomprehension came over his face as nothing came out. This was followed by a look of fury. 'Shit!' he roared. 'Who's drunk my vodka?'

He lifted an arm to throw it to the floor. 'Er Trevor,' I ventured, 'the bottle's full. It's just frozen.'

Keith inspected the bottle closely and looked up. 'Shit!' he roared again. 'You're right! Thanks, mate!' And with that he lurched over to the fridge, grabbed another bottle of vodka and ambled off on his way. I, like the rest of the world, have no idea how Keith manages to behave in the way he does and still stay alive, but that's Keith for you. In late 2001 he had to take a medical for the Stones and was pronounced to be as healthy as a bouncing teenager: his lungs are clear, liver and heart are fine and he'll probably outlive the lot of us. That's unless he really is a vampire, of course, which would explain a good deal.

Keith is far more intelligent than he's usually given credit for, well versed in everything from politics and architecture to natural history. He spends most of his time in the States now, to the extent that he didn't see Redlands, his mansion in West Wittering, Sussex, for eight years. It's a beautiful place, decorated with Tudor beams, 15-foot walls and a moat, but Keith's trips to England from 1986 to 1994 lasted only for a matter of days (for tax reasons – Mick's not the only one who's financially astute) and so he would live in London hotels. On the occasion he set foot in his house after such a long gap, I happened to be driving him. Halfway up the drive he said, 'Kevin, mate, stop the car.'

I did so. Keith leapt out. 'I'm home! I'm home! My beautiful house! I'm home!' he cried and then started doing a dance up the drive waving his rainsticks in the air. As it happened, it was already raining at the time anyway, but Keith, at least, looked pleased with himself.

Keith absolutely adores Redlands and once he is there, he is very difficult to shift. When I went to collect the family after Christmas 2001 to take them to the airport to return home, only Patti and their two daughters, Theodora Dupree and Alexandra Nicole, came out. 'Keith will not be coming with us,' said Patti rather icily and we made off for the airport on our own. After that, I was called to Redlands no less than three times to get Keith to the airport. Each time I would be met with the sheepish reply, 'It's all right, I'm not going.'

The main reason Keith loves Redlands so much is the house itself, but he also loves the lifestyle that goes with it. When Keith is in residence, it's party central with both his long-term girlfriend from the pre-Patti days – Anita Pallenberg – and Marianne Faithfull as regular visitors. Redlands, incidentally, was the scene of the Stones' notorious drug bust in the 1960s, which led to lurid and untrue rumours about a Mars bar, Mick's drug conviction and its subsequent denunciation by the *Times* which famously condemned the courts for breaking a butterfly on a wheel. The house had seen wild times in the past. In those early days, Anita was rumoured to have had flings with both Mick and Marianne, while Marianne claimed that she and Mick were both in love with Keith. She also announced that she and Keith had once had a one-night stand, which Keith denied.

These tensions are all in the past, however. Patti, although not quite as keen on partying as Keith, is completely relaxed about the appearance of friends and lovers from the Sixties, not least because she and Keith have a rock-solid relationship. She does, however, insist that he stay away from Redlands when he's in England, because she knows that once there, it's very hard to get him away. In a short visit in the latter part of 2001, made to see the Stones financial advisor Prince Rupert Lowenstein, he was under specific orders to go nowhere near Redlands. Keith himself is aware of the dangers. 'Got to get a plane before too many people know I'm in town,' he explained gloomily as I drove him to the airport. 'Shit I wish I could stay, but I'm under orders from Patti.'

That said, Patti doesn't wear the trousers in the relationship; it's conducted on an equal footing. They never row, but sometimes Patti does finally put her foot down, and when Patti talks to Keith, he listens. As with Jo and Ronnie, Patti saves Keith from his worst excesses and from his worst enemy – himself.

The local villagers are all very fond of Keith. When he's at Redlands, he can be found most evenings in The Ship Inn, his local, where he is well known and well liked. He made a generous donation of £30,000 to the local church to mark the millennium, and he even gets on well with the local police – in marked contrast to his early days. They keep an eye on the house for him when he's away and visit him in their Panda car when he's back. Keith plies them with tea and gets all the local gossip, while swigging back the vodka himself.

It's a well-known fact that the Stones have houses littered all over the world; what is not so widely known is that the same applies to cars. Mick has two Ferraris stored away in England and one in France, although as he says, he can only drive the one in France. 'The last time me and Jerry went out in the Ferrari in England,' he once told me, 'it nearly caused a riot. People notice cars like that in England. They're cooler in France.' Keith also has a number of cars stashed away all over the place – so many so that he had completely forgotten about a car he had bought in 1966, a Bentley S10 which had been in storage for years near Alexandra Palace, on the outskirts of London. One day by chance, member of his office was rummaging through records and found the car: 'Shit!' roared Keith, when it was brought to his attention. 'Let's have it out!'

I was put in charge of liberating the car from storage. It

had changed colours several times over the years and was now leaf green with a very thin line running right down the body and over the hub caps. That line is made up of the Rastafarian colours, red, green and yellow, a reference to Keith's love of Jamaica, where he first went when he was with Anita Pallenberg. The inside is as it's always been, covered with beige leather.

I drove it to the airport to collect Keith, who was overjoyed to see his motor again. He clambered in with an evil look on his face and started rummaging around in the glove compartment. 'Have you seen this?' he demanded, producing a microphone.

'What's so great about a microphone?' I asked.

'There's an amplifier and a speaker under the grill,' said Keith, looking more evil still. 'It means I can say what I want to the people outside. Let's have some fun!' Unfortunately – or perhaps fortunately – the car had been in storage for so long that the microphone no longer worked and the passers-by on the way from Heathrow to Sussex never found out what Keith had to say about them.

Keith is a very generous man, but also an impractical one. When his daughter by Anita Pallenberg, Angela, got married to her boyfriend, carpenter Dominic Jennings in 1998 when she was twenty-six, Keith laid on an extremely grand wedding for her at Redlands. The rest of the Stones were present, apart from Mick who was out of the country. It was a wild occasion, with each guest attempting to out drink the next, while the bride herself turned down her father's offer to sing at the nuptials. 'Keith asked her if she would like the band to play for her but she wasn't keen and the matter was dropped,' reported journalist Rick Sly at the time.

Keith's present to the happy couple was a brand new Land Rover Discovery, which was standing in pride of place at Redlands, covered with bows and ribbons and looking cute – if a Land Rover can be said to look cute. The couple stayed at West Wittering for a few days after the ceremony and then returned to Dartford with the Land Rover in tow. The only trouble was that Angela was not yet eligible to drive as she was still taking lessons for her licence, while Dominic had lost his licence after a drink-driving charge. Keith's divorced parents, Doris and Bert were at the wedding, as well as Doris's second husband Bill and it was the latter who realised there might be a problem. After an investigation, Keith's office contacted me. 'We need you to go and pick up the car,' they said, and so I drove the car to Allan Dunn, a long-time associate of Mick, who lived in the country. Angela lost her nerve and never completed her driving lessons, and so the car remained in situ until Dominic's ban was over and he was allowed to take possession of the car again.

Cars are an issue with Keith. When the new Volkswagen Beetle came out he bought one – and was promptly infuriated to discover there were no ashtrays in it. He was so annoyed that he nearly wrote a letter to the company. 'No!' he roared. 'Why can't I have a smoke in my own car!' Such was his annoyance, that the car ended up with his two younger daughters.

Keith is exceptionally generous to all his children and especially to Marlon, his oldest child. In 1999 Marlon was staying in Redlands with Anita at the time of his birthday. I was sent by his father to take him presents: the presents included bottles of champagne, wrapped gifts and one very special item – an envelope containing £10,000 in cash. Keith might not be a very conventional father but no one can accuse him of not caring about his children, in his own inimitable way.

**3**

# The Way They Were

THE FIRST TIME I met Mick and Jerry was in 1989 when I was driving the band Living Colour, who had supported The Rolling Stones on the 'Steel Wheels' tour. I got a quick glimpse of the two of them, but little more: even in that fleeting moment, though, they managed to come across as possibly the most glamorous couple in the world. *I wonder if I'll ever get to know them better*, I thought, but soon forgot all about such ideas.

The next time I met them was a couple of years later, when I went to the house they were then renting in Notting Hill. I was asked to collect a parcel and their then driver asked me in to have a cup of tea. When I was sitting in the kitchen,

Jerry wandered in and began to heat up some leftover pasta for her lunch. It was our first real meeting and the thing that struck me most at the time was that Jerry Hall was absolutely stunning. She was also extremely warm and sociable. 'How are you Keith?' she said. 'I'm Jerry.' She tipped the pasta in to a bowl and wandered off. This was also my first experience of Jerry's very healthy appetite. She doesn't need to watch her weight – she eats like a horse.

Gradually I began to drive the family around more. I started taking the two of them to restaurants on a regular basis. Then Mick decided he wanted a place in the country. So we began to have a look at places around Reading and Canterbury before he finally decided that, actually, Richmond was far enough out of London for him. I got on increasingly well with the Jaggers and after a while, I found I was driving them almost all of the time.

Back when I first knew them, Mick and Jerry were a truly loving married couple. They used to kiss and cuddle all the time and Mick was always making romantic gestures. He would send Jerry flowers at least once a week, enormous bouquets made up of gorgeous, brightly coloured exotic flowers, or sometimes dozens of lilies and roses. He would also buy her items of jewellery from Philips, a jewellers on Bond Street in London, and a place he still goes to every Christmas. Mick was also always interested in Jerry's

51

appearance. Going through magazines, he would rip out pages and pass them across to her saying, 'Maybe you could do something with that look.'

Looking back, I cannot for the life of me understand why Mick treated Jerry the way he did, for the very simple reason that he genuinely loved her – and still does, according to many people. The pair first met back in 1976 when Jerry was just twenty. Mick was still married to his first wife – Bianca – at the time, and Jerry was at the time ensconced with her first rock star, Roxy Music singer Bryan Ferry. The two – Bryan and Jerry – had met in 1975 when Bryan saw pictures of Jerry in *Vogue* and decided she would be perfect to model for the cover of Roxy's next album, *Siren*. Jerry, who was then based in New York, was just making her name as a model: she came over to Britain for the shoot and together with fashion designer Anthony Price, the couple made their way down to Wales.

The shoot has actually gone down in rock music history because of the problems involved in getting Jerry's costume off. She was to be dressed up as a mermaid and so wore a tiny blue bikini, long blonde wig, false eyelashes, blue fingernails and was painted from top to toe in blue body paint. She had little wings glued on to her ankles and little fins glued on to her body and the overall result, when it finally appeared, was spectacular.

But there was a series of problems during the shoot, the first being that the weather was boiling hot, which meant the glue on Jerry's body started to melt and bits kept falling off. Then, when the pictures had been taken, a further problem emerged: Jerry couldn't get rid of the blue body paint. Not only that, but there was only one more train that day back to London and if the party didn't catch it, they'd be stuck in a little town in Wales overnight. So Bryan and Anthony wrapped Jerry in towels and literally carried her on to the train in order to speed back to town. Once on the train, she tried to get the blue gunk off – again without success, and so she had to be whisked back to Bryan's house that night. And so began her romance with one of the most stylish men in rock music.

Jerry went on to do a lot more with Bryan both personally and professionally: she also appeared in the video for 'Let's Stick Together' – as we now know, they didn't – and she moved to London to be with him before the two ended up getting engaged when they were on holiday in the Caribbean. Jerry has always been very generous about Bryan. She has commented on his exquisite taste in art and antiques and the fact that she started to learn a great deal from him about both of those subjects, as well as about literature and all-round good living. But then circumstances combined to change their lives.

For a start, Jerry herself has written about the fact that she felt very constrained by Bryan, who apparently was embarrassed by her penchant for leg wrestling in public and generally whooping it up as a high-living Texan gal. And then Bryan did something that was extremely unwise: he accepted an invitation from Mick Jagger to attend a Rolling Stones concert – with, of course, his lovely fiancée – and to go and meet the band backstage afterwards. After that initial meeting, everyone went off to dinner and back to Bryan's house afterwards: Jerry and Mick sat together in the back of a limousine and Mick signalled his interest by firmly pressing his leg against Jerry's. Jerry responded in kind.

From then on, it was just a matter of time. Back at Bryan's place that night, Mick pursued Jerry openly and unashamedly: she, however, aware that Bryan was watching them, attempted to put him off. Bryan finally got so sick of the whole proceedings that he went off to bed. He turned down all invitations to meet Mick after that, furious at Mick's attempts to seduce Jerry and there it might have ended were it not for the fact that a couple of months later, Bryan went off on a two-month tour of Australia and Japan. Jerry actually wanted to accompany him, but Bryan vetoed this idea for reasons best known to himself – and further announced that he wouldn't be able to phone her for those two months because it would be too expensive. A thoroughly exasperated Jerry returned to New York to take up her modelling career while he was away, bumped in to Mick ... and the rest, as they say, is history.

And Mick and Jerry made total sense together as a couple: he was the greatest rock musician of his generation and she was the greatest model of hers. They caused a sensation wherever they went. Jerry was impossibly beautiful and glamorous and Mick was the absolute essence of cool. By all accounts Mick was actually faithful to her for the first couple of years that they were together and when he did resume his philandering, he did not make it as public as it was later to become. The couple set up home together almost immediately. Jerry gave birth to Elizabeth Scarlett in 1984, followed by James Leroy Augustin the following year. Mick and Jerry finally married in a ceremony in Bali in 1990 and two more children followed: Georgia May Ayeesha in 1992 and Gabriel Luke Beauregard five years later.

In the beginning of the 1980s, though, Mick began to show signs of restlessness. Jerry dealt with this by promptly going out with the millionaire racehorse owner Robert Sangster who, as she once remarked, could buy Mick out a hundred times over. That brought Mick to heel and they were quickly reconciled. 'I did that to punish Mick,' she told an interviewer after they were reconciled following the affair in 1982. 'He was dallying with some little blue-blood East

Coast tramp playing heaven knows what under a table so I though I'd play him at his own dirty little game.'

For years the two of them maintained a happy relationship until the advent of the Italian model Carla Bruni, with whom Mick had an on-again off-again affair for some years. Jerry threatened divorce proceedings in 1996, but backed off and gave it one last go. Until the advent of Luciana Morad, the affair with Carla signalled the closest point that Mick and Jerry had come to breaking up and it has been widely reported that Gabriel was a second honeymoon baby, designed to get the marriage back on track. Very sadly, it didn't work.

That said, the good times were very good indeed. Mick and Jerry would go out a lot together, to restaurants, shows and private parties. Weekends would be spent with friends such as Lord Channing and Paul Getty in the country. The restaurants they liked to go to included The Ivy, still one of Mick's favourites, Claridges and Mr Chow and friends came from all over the place: the world of modelling, rock 'n' roll and the real aristocracy, which both Jerry and Mick adore.

Both are collectors and would attend auctions either together or separately and then bid on one another's behalf. Mick in particular loves paintings: he would leave catalogues in the back of the car with ticks against the pictures he wanted to bid for. One particular favourite is Andy Warhol and he also has a couple of paintings by Prince Charles. I recall that in the back of the car he would frequently be on the phone to auction houses, and I've known him to spend £250,000 in the course of one afternoon.

Mick never dressed well except for special occasions, but still there was an aura of glamour and sophistication about he and Jerry, the kind of aura that is produced by true charisma. Mick would wear jeans, plimsolls, baseball boots and trainers, while Jerry would look heart-stoppingly beautiful in whatever she was wearing. Mick liked the fact that she was a top model and would often buy clothes for her, as well as jewellery. This empathy with women is one of the factors that makes him so alluring to the opposite sex. Despite Mick's casual dress sense he was – and is – clearly powerfully attractive to women. His personality oozes sex appeal. Mick's an incredibly attractive man when he's in a good mood – his whole face lights up and his beautiful eyes become captivating.

When Mick's in a bad mood, he goes very quiet and becomes sharp and to the point. His face becomes very stern. But he's not often in a bad mood with women. He quite genuinely loves female company so much that, unlike so many men, he's come to understand how the female mind works. The down side of Mick is that he can be very selfish, and that's not only by cheating on the women in his life. He never gets nasty and he's always been fair to me, but he can bark out instructions abruptly, fail to clarify them, snap down the phone and then hang up if any pleasantries are attempted.

He is also, however, incredibly loyal. Two weeks before Christmas in 1997, when Jerry was pregnant with Gabriel, I dropped Jerry off at the osteopath and then went on to a shop in west London to collect some ballet slippers for her, as she'd decided they'd be comfortable to wear around the house. On the way there I got stuck in traffic. Then, out of the blue, a young man leapt in to the road, opened the passenger door of the car in front and grabbed a woman's bag. The woman held on and the man was dragged back in to the car. I grabbed the keys out of the ignition of my car, leapt out and went after him. There was a nasty struggle: he pulled a knife, but I hit him twice, got him out of the car and threw him up against a van. He was wearing a big puffa jacket; he wriggled out of that and ran off.

I'd had the car in neutral, but it was on an incline and rolled down, crashing in to the car in front – the car from which the bag had been grabbed. The driver, incidentally, seemed a lot more angry about her car being bumped than grateful for the fact that I'd helped her, but there you are. By this time, though, I was getting late, so I gave the woman my card, got the ballet slippers and drove back to collect Jerry.

When she came out she saw that the front of the car was all smashed up and that my hands were covered in blood: 'Honey, what happened?' she asked, a picture of concern, in that lovely Southern drawl of hers. When I told her, she said, 'But Keith, why did you get out of the car?'

'Because I'm a man, Jerry. I felt I had to.'

'You could have been killed. You should have been more careful,' she cautioned me, as we drove on back to Richmond.

Jerry clearly told Mick about the incident because he knew exactly what to expect when I turned up the next day as planned to take him Christmas shopping. My car was still badly damaged and looked a sight. 'Look Mick, I'm really sorry that I've got to drive you in to town, no one else is free,' I explained. 'But from noon you'll have another car.'

'Why?' asked Mick. 'Can you get nicked for driving a car in that condition?'

'No, it's not that,' I said. 'But Mick, imagine what will happen if the paparazzi get a shot of you getting out of a smashed-up car. You'd never hear the end of it.'

'Fuck them,' he replied, getting in the car. 'I want to be driven in this one. Let's go.' And for the next two weeks he insisted I drive him around in my battered old motor as a display of loyalty to me. Then again, it may have been just another example of Mick's notorious control freakery. Over time he became quite possessive about making sure it was always me who drove him – so much so that it quite put the other Stones' noses out of joint.

Mick was always very protective of Jerry back then, always making sure that she was safe, happy, looked after and protected from the people around her. He was very gentlemanly, ushering her through doors first and in to the car before him. The only occasion in all the years I've driven them that I have ever seen him get really angry was when I took them both to a charity function in the mid-1990s at a famous restaurant in London. Usually on these occasions I look after the couple myself, but this time the security men on the door assured me they would do it for me.

Wherever Mick and Jerry go, the rest of London follows. Word got out that they were in the restaurant and soon quite a big crowd had built up outside the door. Mick and Jerry emerged, but instead of being escorted by the guards to the car, they were left on their own in the middle of the crowd, being jostled to and fro. I tried to get out to help but there was a crush around the car as well and I couldn't get the doors open.

Eventually Mick got Jerry to the car. He pushed her in, stumbled in after her and then whirled round on his seat, kicking out with his feet at the crowd – which even then was trying to push its way in to the car. 'Fuck off, just fuck off,' he roared, before Jerry pulled him inside and got the door shut. 'Why the fuck did that happen!' yelled Mick as we finally drove off. 'Where were those fucking security guards! Why the fuck didn't they look after us?' The two of them were clearly extremely shaken by their ordeal and glad to get away.

Mick and Jerry often held dinner parties and birthday parties for themselves and the children. There was also an annual Christmas party in Richmond and an annual New Year's Eve party in Mustique, which everyone would attend in fancy dress. Mick would lay on surprises for his beautiful wife: once he hired a boat and took Jerry, the children and a selection of friends and relatives on the river.

Jerry and her fellow model and best friend Marie Helvin would sometimes go to Cliveden, the luxurious country house hotel that had been the scene of the notorious Profumo scandal back in the 1960s, and which now looks after the rich and famous in a very different way. The two of them would go to use the hotel's luxurious spa for numerous beauty treatments, although to be honest, they always looked exactly the same to me afterwards as they had done before. Neither of them suffer from any kind of eating disorder, though, as so many girls today seem to; both women have very healthy appetites. On one occasion, as we were driving down, there was a shout from the back of the car. 'Ooh Marie,' said Jerry. 'Let's stop for fish and chips!' I drove them to a nearby chippy and procured their food for them before driving on as the former Miss World and the world's greatest supermodel delved in to their newspaper-wrapped lunch in the back of the car.

The couple would always make an effort to attend their children's school sports days. At the beginning of the 1990s, both Elizabeth and James were at Ibstock School in Richmond and Jerry would take a big hamper for a picnic there. Jerry absolutely loves picnics. She would make a huge fuss about the food – 'Ooh, look, Mick, at what Yvette's packed!' There would be cucumber and salmon sandwiches, chicken legs, big bags of Kettles chips, which Jerry adores, biscuits and home-made cakes, fruit and water.

Elizabeth and James both regularly took part in school sports. James, in particular, is very sporty and loves cricket, rugby and soccer. Mick was always asked to take part in the adults races; he would say yes to the 100 metres and a very big no to the egg and spoon and sack races. The other parents would treat Mick quite normally and he would mingle with them and chat to the masters, but he would always find a spot not too close to the others to sit down for the picnic. The children, meanwhile, would be scampering around with their friends, aware that their parents stood out from the crowd and not altogether unhappy about the fact.

There is constant comedy in being a celebrity parent. Shortly after Gabriel was born, Mick went shopping with his wardrobe mistress to pick out clothes for the Stones' 'Bridges of Babylon' tour. Jerry decided to come along for the shopping and brought Gabriel, whom she was still breastfeeding. In the middle of Walton Street there was suddenly an explosion of smell from the back of the car. 'Phew!' roared Mick. 'What the fuck's that?'

It was, of course, little Gabriel, needing his nappy to be changed. I drove along as Jerry set about changing him while Mick, complaining vociferously though goodheartedly, rolled down the window and stuck his head out. As always, a crowd gathered immediately at the sight of Mick Jagger's head suddenly popping out of a limo. I was driving slowly so that Jerry could change Gabriel, so the crowd was able to follow our progress.

'All right Mick, how you doing!' someone cried.

'I'm all right, how are you? Comin' to the next set of shows?'

'Yeah, Mick! When are they?'

'We're just planning the new tour,' Mick replied. And so our strange procession went on: the latest Jagger offspring being changed in the car and the icon himself drawing the crowds with him as he hung out of it. Eventually Jerry was done and she passed me the dirty nappy, I deposited it in a rubbish bin and we were off again, to the great disappointment of Mick's many adoring fans. Mick and Jerry went off to lunch after that, incidentally, and I did my stuff in the car with the air freshener. On another occasion, Jerry and a friend were both in the car breastfeeding on either side of Mick. 'Oh, put them away,' he quipped.

Another annual occasion that the family used to enjoy was Sir Paul Getty's cricket matches. Sir Paul has a house near High Wycombe, with his own cricket team. It's set in thousands of acres and has a full-sized cricket pitch with its own pavilion; in the distance you could see exotic Afghan cattle and thousands of sheep. I'd drive the whole family up including Mick's parents Eva – who is sadly no longer with us – and Joe.

It would be a very splendid affair. Drinks would flow all day and a girl would ride round on a push bike with a big box of ice cream on the front, just as they used to in the 1950s. Prince Charles was a regular visitor, along with many members of the aristocracy, something which Mick loves – he prefers old money to new. Sir Paul's team would play Eton, Windsor or even some England players; equally, when teams from South Africa, the West Indies and Australia were over, some would play against Sir Paul's team. Mick absolutely loves cricket and although he doesn't play much himself, he does do commentaries.

Another regular destination was Guinness castle in Ireland. Mick is friends with the Guinness sisters, Sabrina and Miranda; the latter works in his office. The Jaggers would visit the castle once a year and back in London would frequently have dinner with the sisters and their friends. They would also go and stay on other friends' yachts.

Mick's father Joe is enormously proud of his son. He accompanied Mick, Jerry and the children to open the Mick Jagger Performing Arts Centre, when it opened in 2000 at Mick's alma mater, Dartford Grammar School. Mick was very excited by the occasion, joking to students, 'I'll see if the bike sheds are still here.' (Mick does far more for charity than he's given credit for.) On this occasion in particular there were tears in Joe's eyes. 'I'm so very proud, seeing this building named after my son,' he said to me, visibly moved.

But such domestic serenity was not to last. Throughout this idyllic period, Mick never once gave up seeing other women and nothing and no one could stop him. Jerry would give interviews, telling of the pain his infidelity caused and describing how dreadful it felt when she found another woman's earring by their bed, but still Mick philandered on. There were long-term affairs, such as the one with the Italian model Carla Bruni, and one-night stands. There were regular girlfriends and sudden conquests.

Mick has a particular partiality for models and, as Jerry

herself remarked, he always wanted the new one on the scene. For many years, he would get her. Often and inevitably these flings would find their way in to the newspapers and Mick would, in his own way, try to make amends. He would send Jerry faxes with 'I love you' written on them, go on extravagant shopping sprees to buy her clothes and jewellery, wine her, dine her and woo her as if they were still young lovers rather than a couple who had been together for more than twenty years.

But Mick could not bring himself to give up other women. One night he would tell Jerry he wanted the two of them to be together forever; the next night he'd be out with a model young enough to be his granddaughter. It stretched Jerry's tolerance to breaking point and beyond and finally, when it emerged that yet another model, Luciana Morad, had borne Mick a child, the strain finally became too much and she cracked.

No one who knows Mick can understand his behaviour. Jerry was unquestionably the love of his life and his actions are not motivated by hatred of women – quite the opposite. In the end, I believe it is Mick who has been the loser and Jerry who will end up happy, but it sometimes seemed as if subconsciously he was determined to destroy the relationship. And, very sad to say, he succeeded.

# You Can't
# Always Get What
# You Want

I FIRST REALISED that something was seriously wrong between Mick and Jerry back in 1998. I had driven Mick to a party at The Hempel Hotel in west London and sent another car to collect Jerry from Richmond. The idea was that the other car would then go home and I'd drive the couple back together.

After I dropped Mick off, I went to dismiss my other driver. 'But Keith,' he said, 'Jerry told me to wait. She said she'd be leaving at ten.' It was very odd and very unlike Jerry, but there was nothing I could do. 'Okay,' I said, 'you'd better wait.'

At ten Jerry appeared, got in the car and drove off. An

hour later Mick came out. 'Have you seen Jerry?' he demanded.

'Yes, she's gone,' I told him.

'How? Did she get a cab?'

'No, she kept her car on.'

As he began to realise that Jerry had planned an early getaway without him, Mick began to look a little bemused. There were photographers all over the place, though, so there was nothing he could do right away. Instead, he got in the car, we drove off and then he got me to stop again round the corner. 'Keith,' he said, 'can you phone the driver and ask where he took her?'

I did so. 'He thought it was a little hotel,' I reported back.

Mick whipped out his mobile and started making a call. When there was no answer, he began to get increasingly annoyed and agitated, jumping up and down on the back seat of the car. 'Keith, ring the driver again and find out exactly where he took her,' he ordered.

It was an address in central London. Mick calmed down a little when he heard that and instructed me to take him back to Richmond, but then started getting angry and upset again when he repeatedly tried to call Jerry and continued to get no reply. When we got back to the house, he got out of the car without a word, slammed the door behind him and stalked off. *Something is really wrong*, I thought.

It was soon after that incident that rumours began to circulate that Brazilian model Luciana Morad was pregnant with Mick's child. Jerry hit the roof and Mick finally began to realise, for the very first time, that he had gone too far. The rows were violent and frequently public. 'You're a fifty-five-year-old man who has fathered four children with me. How can you humiliate them and continue to humiliate me?' she asked him.

Mick denied everything and swore it wasn't his child, but Jerry had had enough. For years she had had to put up with Carla Bruni lurking in the background and the discovery that Mick had actually fathered another woman's child was just too much. I think she felt for the children, too. It has since emerged that they were getting teased at school and it must have been an extraordinarily difficult time for them as well as their mother.

Unusually for her, Jerry became quite vicious in her denunciation of Mick. She told him that he was 'deluded' about still being sexually attractive and that he was 'no Peter Pan'. M'learned friends were summoned on to the scene: Jerry roped in Princess Diana's divorce lawyer, Anthony Julius, and his US associate, Raoul Fedler.

The *Sun*, which broke the news about Morad's pregnancy, reported soon afterwards that Jerry ran crying in to her home after waving off dinner guests when a bodyguard handed her an early copy of the newspaper on Thursday night. It contained an interview with a friend of the couple who stated that Mick was 'in pieces and Jerry absolutely hit the roof. He knows that Luciana's lump could cost him half of everything he owns. He and Jerry have had rows before over women – but there's never been a baby involved. For the first time I think Mick realises that this could be the final straw for him and Jerry. She could put up with his womanising and the fact that he's always jetting off around the world, but the pregnancy is a different matter.'

And then, to my utter astonishment, everyone calmed down. For a very brief time Mick and Jerry seemed to get back to normal as Mick point-blank denied the rumours and begged his beautiful companion to remain by his side. They were going out together less, however, and the only time Jerry was really affectionate towards him was when she'd had a couple of glasses of wine, when she'd snuggle up to him in the back of the car and they'd kiss and cuddle as they had done so many times before.

Luciana, meanwhile, was equally insistent that the baby was Mick's. 'She said Mick was wonderful in bed – very considerate and loving,' said one of her friends in one of numerous interviews that was given before the baby was born. 'But she said the weird thing was he insisted on making love without a condom and didn't even ask if she was on the Pill … the truth is that she has told us she is pregnant by Mick Jagger.' Another friend chimed in: 'Luciana has told everyone she … is going to keep the child. She is determined the baby should be recognised as Mick's and wants it to have his surname.'

Mick and Jerry soldiered on. But any hope of long-lasting reconciliation went down the drain in May 1999, when Luciana's son Lucas was born and Mick turned out indeed to be the father. It was a surprise to no one – except, perhaps, Jerry, and my heart went out to her; she was absolutely distraught. Now the real rows began: terrible screaming matches as Jerry berated Mick for his behaviour. 'An affair is just an affair,' she would cry, 'but this is a baby.' It was a dreadful time for Jerry. Her twin sister Terri, to whom she is very close, had just been diagnosed with breast cancer and Jerry was spending much of her time in Texas to help her recover. Back in England, meanwhile, she was sinking in to an increasingly bad depression.

Still Mick tried to win Jerry back, taking her out to dinner, wooing her and promising to settle down with her and the children. He was so persistent that at one point it looked as if he had succeeded. To celebrate their reunion he sent Jerry a huge bunch of flowers and bought her a piece of jewellery from Philips.

It was a very short reconciliation, though, and for a very

good reason: Mick was still seeing all his other women. 'If you mean what you say,' said Jerry, when he made yet another promise to mend his ways, 'then you wouldn't still be doing what you're doing.' Even Mick's friends were disgusted by his behaviour: 'He's old enough to keep it in his trousers by now,' said one.

Finally the situation came to a head. 'Keith, I need you to bring me a car,' Mick told me on the phone one day. 'Make it a basic one, nothing too flashy.'

I rented a Volvo estate and drove to the back of the house, where Mick was waiting for me with a suitcase and a couple of bags. We stashed the bags in the car and then Mick hid under the cover that went down across the bag. We drove past the hordes of waiting photographers, who were still waiting for Mick to go past in a Bentley, drove round the corner, where he climbed out from the back and then on to The Dorchester, where he rented a suite for a couple of weeks. He was extremely subdued on that journey. I didn't say anything. What was there to say?

And from that day to this, Mick has been a changed man. He can still be lively in company, forever the Jumpin' Jack Flash at the centre of attention wherever he is in the world. But in private, Mick is quieter than he used to be. Where once he was a cocky rock star, always up for it (whatever 'it' may be) at any time of the day or night, these days there's a melancholic streak in his character. Mick will never, ever admit he was wrong, especially when it comes to his own sexual fidelity, but I suspect that sometimes he wonders whether it was all worth it. Yes, he still beds beautiful women, but he's lost the close family life he once so enjoyed.

And Mick's getting older now, too. Not every woman in the world wants to be just another notch on his bedpost and the refusals are becoming quite as common as the acceptances with the women he propositions. One woman he bumps in to regularly says that these days his preferred method of wooing is to send text messages; it gives the illusion of youth on the part of the sender and makes it easier to fool himself that if there is no answer, the message hasn't arrived. But Mick's a grandfather these days and increasingly out of touch with the world he used to inhabit. In the documentary *Being Mick*, he said that he would rather go out and enjoy himself than sit around in a pub saying he used to be big in the Sixties, but perhaps even Mick realises there was a third alternative – one that involved Jerry and a happy family life.

But there was no going back now. Jerry had finally done what she had never done before and forced Mick to move out. And Mick quickly developed a new routine. I'd go to pick him up at about lunchtime and drive him and his personal trainer to Hyde Park to exercise. Then it was back to The Dorchester, a quick shower and off to Richmond, where I'd sneak him in to the house in the trunk of the car. He'd stay there with the children until about eight and then it was off to dinner as normal. Jerry became increasingly depressed during this period. She was often on the verge of tears and would snap at just about anything.

Even Mick began to buckle under the pressure. The house was normally besieged by paparazzi, but on one occasion there was just a father and son team waiting outside. Mick proceeded to behave in a way I have never seen him behave before or since. He went ballistic. 'Is this the way you bring your son up!' he screamed as he chased after the father. 'Snooping around in other people's lives!'

After a few weeks at The Dorchester, Mick went home. The family had always had the flat in the house next door but now Mick moved in to it full time. He went out more than ever, seeing more women than ever, in an attempt to take his mind off the rift with Jerry, but nothing worked. He seemed to become frenzied; he would go from one woman to the next in the course of one night, but still the problem wouldn't go away. Mick wouldn't give up the other women and so, at long last, his relationship with Jerry – a relationship of twenty-three years' standing – finally fell apart.

Both of them were badly shocked when Jerry filed for

divorce, although for different reasons. Mick simply couldn't believe that Jerry really was going to leave him after all this time. Jerry, on the other hand, was devastated when she discovered that their 1991 marriage in Bali was not legal. Nor were matters helped by the fact that Luciana was launching her own claim for child support: an initial demand of £32,000 a month. In the end it was whittled down to a seven-figure lump son and £5,000 a month.

Jerry was fighting for her own settlement. After the marriage was declared null by the High Court, she was awarded about £10 million. The house remained in both names and Jerry was given permission to live there, but if she remarries, she'll have to move out. Mick pays all the joint bills and those pertaining to the children, but Jerry pays for anything she wants for herself.

For some months the atmosphere was dreadful. Mick spent time at his chateau in France and rented a flat in Paris, coming back at weekends to see the children. Jerry grew increasingly depressed; she was smoking more than ever and always complaining about what had happened to her and the most important relationship in her life. People have often wondered why Jerry stayed with Mick for as long as she did, but the reason isn't so hard to work out: she genuinely thought she'd be the one to change him, to make him settle down. It was some time before she could accept the fact that this wasn't going to happen. Mick Jagger was never going to change for anyone, not even Jerry Hall.

And then, quite suddenly, the atmosphere began to lighten. They say that to get over one man you should get under another and that is just what Jerry did: she started a relationship with the film producer George Waud. The relationship was not to last but it was exactly what she needed at the time – some solid love and affection. And so the fight back at Mick began.

Jerry decided she wanted Mick out and she wanted him out now. To that end, she kicked off an almost comical series of attempts to show Mick that he wasn't welcome. The first occurred just before Mick was due back from a trip abroad. Jerry assembled the staff. 'I want you all to leave the house for a few hours,' she told them.

'When Mick comes back and knocks on the door, I know you all would have to open the door for him,' she continued. 'Well, I don't have to.' Everyone left the house, Jerry barricaded all the doors and when Mick returned he found himself barred from the house, left out on the street to be chuckled at by the neighbours. Eventually Jerry relented and allowed him back in, but not before Mick realised that he was no longer wanted in what once had been his home.

Mick has always been close to his children, but he's a man who likes his lie-in and he doesn't usually get home until two or three in the morning. Jerry now started letting Gabriel go in to wake his father – and Gabriel's day begins shortly after eight. He rushes in with screams of joy, eager to play with Daddy, and Daddy must oblige. Nor is Daddy likely to get much sympathy from Mummy should he be unwise enough to complain. It's almost possible to feel sorry for the poor man.

On yet another occasion, Mick returned home to find that someone had put the chain on the inside of the front door to his flat. He came out, walked around to Jerry's front door in order to get access through the dining room and found that someone had put the inside chain on that, too. Eventually, by means of a series of phone calls in which he harangued everyone he could think of, Mick gained entrance somehow, but again the neighbours were treated to the sight of their famous neighbour exiled out in the street. Another time, the electronic gates were turned off inside the house, which meant that I couldn't drive in and Mick was forced to climb over the wall.

Perhaps surprisingly, through all this Mick, Jerry and the children have remained on good terms. There probably always was the possibility that the couple would be reunited until Jerry met Tim, with whom she is genuinely in love. She has blossomed since the dark days of the divorce: she's happy, glowing and laughing again. Tim seems equally devoted to her. As for Mick – he still has a bevy of women running around after him but my guess is that he's still in love with Jerry and always will be.

And he's thrown it away for what? The chance to run around with a group of women young enough to be his granddaughter, none of whom will really be able to satisfy him? Despite everything – Mick's affairs, the fact that Jerry didn't get a very high financial settlement – it's she who's come out as a winner from the divorce. Jerry Hall is still a beautiful woman and she's found love again. Mick's tragedy is that he'll never be able to.

# Thriller — PART I

T HE PLANE HOVE in to view and around me, the enormous crowd began to stir. 'It's him!' called a voice from somewhere deep within the melee. The call was taken up by another fan. 'It's him! It's him!' The excitement was palpable, as more and more members of the crowd took up the chant, 'It's him! It's him! It's Michael! Michael! Michael!'

There were thousands of people mobbing the airport that day in Munich in 1992 as the world's greatest pop star was about to kick off only his second solo tour. And although the crowd was well behaved, there was a kind of feverish anticipation surrounding all of us, me included, as the plane carrying Michael Jackson came in to land. Michael is not only one of the greatest entertainers in the world, but also one of the most mysterious, and we were actually going to see him in person. Little did I know that I was to form a brief friendship with the man himself and get a glimpse behind the scenes of a show business legend.

Back then, though, it was June and the start of Michael's 'Dangerous' tour, a tour that was to break world records and establish him more firmly than ever before as the greatest performer of the age. It was an astonishing endeavour. The first date of the tour was in the Olympic Stadium in Munich on June 27, when Michael performed in front of a sell-out crowd of more than 72,000 people. The tour was scheduled to last a year and a half, finishing in Mexico City in November 1993 and although some of the concerts were cancelled due to Michael's illness, he performed in sixty-seven concerts to approximately 3.5 million people. In the course of it he donated all profits to charity, including his own Heal the World charitable foundation, and his Bucharest concert was sold to HBO for $20 million. This created another world record, as did the recording: it gained the highest audience on any cable channel – 34 per cent – and won the Cable Ace Award. The staging was phenomenal: it took three days to erect and cargo planes had to fly twenty truckloads of equipment in to each country.

As for me, I was about to embark on one of the most exciting adventures of my career. I was to spend four months as one of Michael's drivers and, as his plane taxied towards the airport building, stopped and was instantly surrounded by a police escort, I could hardly contain myself. Nor could the crowd. The cries of, 'Michael! We love you!' had gathered in crescendo to a deafening roar; it felt as though the ground were shaking. That was as nothing, though, as to when the door of the plane opened and Michael stepped out dressed in his usual military garb and red mask and raised a hand to his fans; the noise the crowd made must have reverberated from every tree in the forests of Bavaria. The security just about managed to contain the ecstatic hordes, but they very nearly had mass hysteria on their hands. I have driven some of the biggest names in the business, but I've never seen anything like the public's reaction to Michael Jackson.

To begin with I didn't have anything to do with Michael personally. I was driving his security men around in the third car of the entourage, while Michael usually travelled in a customised minibus luxuriously kitted out with facilities for eating and sleeping. Right from the start, though, you could tell he was no ordinary superstar. Everywhere we went, roads and traffic were blocked off for his arrival, a police escort drove us through the cities and the crowds went absolutely wild. We didn't have an escort for our three-strong convoy between the cities, though, which led to one potentially nasty incident.

Michael was in the van and another driver, Stan, and I were following behind in two cars. Suddenly my walkie-talkie bleeped. 'Keith,' said Stan, 'what's that coming up behind us?'

I looked in my rear view mirror and at first I saw what looked like a couple of motorcycles. Then a couple of more joined them and a couple more until there were several dozen in pursuit – and it suddenly hit me with a jolt that we were being followed by a gang of forty or fifty German bikers. 'I don't like this, Stan,' I said in to my walkie-talkie. 'We'd better get the minibus to speed up.'

All three of us put our feet on the accelerators, but the bikers were gaining on us and it wasn't long before we were surrounded. After another minute, they'd got their bikes in between the various cars in an attempt to separate us. The situation was getting pretty frightening. Then my walkie-talkie bleeped again. 'What we're going to do is this,' said Stan. 'You go as close to the curb as you can on your side and I'll do the same on the other side. Then we'll come in sharply behind Michael's bus in a V and cut him off from the bikes.' We did exactly that and it worked: the bikers were forced to slow down. They were furious, yelling curses at us, spitting and trying to get in between us all again, but this time we didn't falter. I kept my car exactly two inches behind Michael's bus and Stan drove exactly two inches behind me until at last the bikers got tired of the chase and turned back to create havoc elsewhere. Michael was asleep at the time; he never knew what had happened.

I still hadn't properly met Michael, though, and it was only because of a near disaster, for which I thought I'd be dismissed, that we actually became friendly. Michael was staying in Rome and wanted to go to Florence to look at a picture he was considering buying. There were something like 2,000 fans in front of the hotel, however, and getting him out of the hotel and on the road would be no easy matter. So his security people formulated a plan. Various cars were stationed at various exits from the hotel, while Michael's official car and police escort was round at the front. The choice of which car to take would be made at the very last minute. Suddenly my walkie-talkie bleeped. 'Keith, it's going to be your car,' said Michael's head of security. 'Get ready. We're coming to you.'

I opened the car door and quite suddenly Michael Jackson was beside me. I bundled him and a friend in to the car, while the daughter of the concert promoter got in the front beside me. It took just a couple of seconds for Michael to move between the hotel and the car but in that time he was spotted, screams went up and a moment later the car was surrounded by fans.

There were two security men in front of us: they managed to clear a path between the hysterical bystanders so we could drive off. But just as we were about to move, Michael put his hand on my shoulder. 'Stop!' he cried. 'Someone's taken my friend's hat!'

I stopped, but I wasn't happy. 'It's not safe, Michael,' I said, as the security men frantically waved us on. 'In a crowd like this anything could happen.'

I made to move again. 'Don't go!' cried Michael. 'I want that hat!'

They security men were going ballistic. 'Come on!' yelled one as the crowd roared and surged around us. 'Get going! You've got to move!'

'I'll get you another hat,' said the girl in the seat beside me. 'Please, Michael, we've got to move now.'

Michael finally agreed and so, just as people were beginning to bang on to the car, we moved off. The plan had been to execute a series of right turns to bring us back to the front of the hotel, where we could link up with security, but the traffic was so solid we were forced to turn left in to a one-way street – and we were going the wrong way.

There was no way I could turn round, though, and so, horn blaring and lights flashing, I edged up past the traffic. I then made a few more left turns – and suddenly realised I was totally lost, to say nothing of the fact that I had Michael Jackson in the back of the car and no security men to protect him. For a while I drove around, but it was no good. There was nothing for it: I was going to have to admit what was wrong. 'I'm lost,' I said.

'That's okay,' said Michael in his soft voice. 'What shall we do?'

The girl sitting beside me was not taking things so calmly. 'Get back to the hotel!' she cried. 'You can't drive around Rome with Michael and no security. What if someone recognises him? It could be a calamity!'

She had a point. Michael Jackson is one of the most recognisable people on the planet and the hysteria that surrounds him is such that, even if his fans don't mean to do him any harm, there is a real danger that violence could erupt. Besides, ever since the terrible assassination of John Lennon in New York in 1980, every star has had to be more cautious. The Beatles might have thought they were bigger than Jesus but Michael was arguably bigger than The Beatles at that point in his career. A swift decision was needed.

'Michael,' I said, 'what do you want me to do? I could head for Florence and we could look for the other cars there?'

Michael hesitated. 'I think we'd better go back to the

hotel,' he said eventually and so I turned the car around and we made our way back. Michael was very calm about it, but I thought I could sense that he was getting a little tense. Eventually I found my way back, but now we had a further problem. Michael was lying on the floor of the car when we drove up to the hotel so the fans couldn't see him and mob him, but we were a good 30 feet from the hotel entrance, a path that was blocked by six rows of parked cars, and no security men in sight. 'There's nothing for it, Michael,' I said. 'We're going to have to run for it. Get ready.'

The girl beside me went ahead to alert the hotel. I went round to Michael's door and opened it. Michael leapt out. I threw one arm around him and used the other to ward off the crowd, who nearly had an attack of hysteria when they realised he was in the car after all. We charged through them at speed, got back through the revolving doors in to the hotel, at which point a guard locked the door – and realised that Michael's friend was trapped outside. 'Let him in!' I screamed and the friend got through just before the crowds closed on the hotel.

I went straight upstairs to my hotel room to pack my bags, because I was sure I'd be sent home after that cock-up. A moment later my boss came in. 'What are you doing?' he asked.

'Packing. I'm off home, aren't I?'

'Are you joking?' asked my boss. 'You got him back in to the hotel safely all on your own; it usually takes up to nine security men. Michael is very relieved to be back and he's talking in a very complimentary way about you.'

And so it was that I began a brief friendship with one of the nicest men I have ever known.

The more I got to know him, the more I realised that although Michael Jackson is a brilliant performer, artist and businessman, it's completely true what people say about him: he lost his childhood and he's never been able to make up for that. Despite his business acumen, there's a strange sort of vulnerability about him, which almost makes you want to hug him and tell him to look after himself – and I say that not as a sentimental man. Michael loves toys and toy shops – wherever we went, all over Europe, if we saw a Toys R Us in any given city, we knew that's where we'd end up later.

While we were in London, Michael paid a visit to Hamleys, the famous toy shop on Regent Street, as well as to the Disney shop on the same street. Each shop blacked out its windows so that Michael could look around in private. He spent thousands of pounds on toys; he particularly loves magic sets and he also bought some remote-controlled cars, which he drove up and down the halls in The Dorchester. When we left the shops the whole of the trunk and the back of the car were filled with toys – and apart from a few special ones that he took on with him, they all ended up at children's hospitals, as they did in every city we visited.

Wherever Michael stayed, pinball machines and computer games would be installed in his suite before his arrival. On one occasion he saw a merry-go-round that he liked in a city in Germany, bought it and had it shipped back to his Neverland estate in California. He also had a friend with him on the tour, and having seen the friendship at close hand, I can vouch for the fact that never at any moment was there one tiny signal of impropriety about it.

Everyone knew Michael's friend was with him and everyone accepted it unquestioningly. Our only reservation was that Michael was leaving himself open to innuendo and indeed, that is exactly what happened the following year when it was alleged that he had had improper relationships with young teenagers. It is often forgotten that not one shred of evidence has ever been produced to substantiate those claims.

Having known the man, I didn't believe the allegations then and I don't believe them now. For a start, Michael is such a genuinely nice man that I simply do not believe him capable of the actions of which he's been accused. Secondly, when I was working for him during the 'Dangerous' tour, his attitude towards his friend struck me as simply that of a big brother. He may be a musical genius, but Michael Jackson sometimes has the mentality of a child himself and that is why he loves to play with children. The fact that now that he's got two children of his own – Prince Michael Jackson Jnr and Paris Michael Katherine Jackson – must be the greatest thing in the world for him, because now he can indulge in his love of children's games with his very own offspring.

But despite his enormously likeable and gentle personality, everyone around Michael is frightened of him because of who he is. Michael is aware of this, but doesn't quite know what to do about it. Problems would be reported back to him via Bill Bray his head of security, who has been with him for thirty years, because people just do not dare tell Michael when something has not gone according to plan. It would seem the more famous you are, the more people are scared of you. I can see why they say it's lonely at the top. Bill is one of the few people who isn't scared of Michael and whenever he told him of another case of someone hiding something from him, Michael would say in bewilderment, 'But why doesn't he come and see me himself?' For some reason, though, despite the fact that I was so excited to meet him, I wasn't frightened of him. I treated him normally, which is perhaps why we got on so well.

For a start, he was fascinated by my cockney accent and started trying to mimic it. 'Hello mate, how are you?' he'd say when he got in to the car. 'Hello Michael, how are you?' I'd reply in an attempt at mimicking his own voice – low and very soft – which he would think was great fun.

'Oi, mate!' he'd say.

'Yes Michael?'

'Tell me about cockney rhyming slang.'

So I did. Michael became terribly interested in it for some reason, and got me to start teaching it to him. 'What's the cockney rhyming slang for stairs?' he'd ask.

'Apples and pairs.'

'What's the cockney rhyming slang for suit?'

'Whistle and flute.'

'What's the cockney rhyming slang for cash?'

'Bangers and mash.'

'Oi, mate! That's wild!'

And so it would go on, for hours. Eventually I bought Michael a book about the subject, which he absolutely loved. 'That's great Keith, thank you so much,' he said when I handed it over. He'd sit in the car going through it for hours, giggling when he came across something he particularly liked. One day, he turned to me and announced: 'I'm sitting in a La-Di-Dah!'

'Come again, Michael?'

'La-Di-Dah,' he pronounced triumphantly, before revealing: 'It's a car!'

# 6

# Thriller — PART II

MICHAEL WAS VERY interested in the cities we
visited. When we were actually in situ he tended to
stay in his room because he couldn't go anywhere without
being mobbed, but when we entered a place for the first time
or drove around it on the way to a show, he'd be very
intrigued by these countries, which were so different from
his own. For some reason, he was particularly taken with
Copenhagen. 'Would you like to live here, Keith?' he asked.

'I don't know Michael, I've hardly seen it.'

He mused for a while. Then he announced: 'I want to go
to Tivoli Park.'

And so, after he'd done his concerts, we arranged for him

to visit Tivoli Park, Copenhagen's foremost amusement park, on the last day of his stay. The visit was to be on a Sunday and the arrangements were very hush-hush because we didn't want to attract the usual hordes that surround Michael wherever he goes. We planned to smuggle him in at a side entrance and spend an afternoon there. Michael was extremely excited by the whole thing.

His excitement turned to shock and then disappointment when we got there, though, because the side gate through which he was to slip in opened to reveal banks of photographers, cheerleaders and a band. His first inclination was to turn back and it took us a good fifteen minutes to persuade him to go in after all, but once there he began to enjoy himself. I drove him from one ride to the next – he couldn't walk between them because he'd be mobbed – and his reactions were like those of an excited child. 'Wow, that was fantastic!' he'd say on re-entering the car. 'I loved that!' He enjoyed the ride on which you were whirled round in buckets so much that he insisted on going on it twice and asked me to come on it with him, too.

'I can't Michael, I've got to watch the car,' I'd tell him.

'Aw, Keith, you're no fun!'

As ever, though, it took no time at all for word to get around that Michael Jackson was in the park and crowds soon began to gather. Michael reluctantly decided after an hour that he'd have to leave rather than spending the whole afternoon there as planned, so instead we got a local driver to take us to the city's military and souvenir shops. Michael loved those. He spent about two hours in one of them, buying up more of the bright uniforms he so loves to wear.

It was Michael's birthday during the tour and we held a birthday party for him in the grounds of his hotel in Frankfurt. We had a barbecue and people relaxed on the sunny lawn as we serenaded him with 'Happy Birthday'. Michael didn't come to the barbecue himself, because every time he was in public, he'd be besieged by fans, but someone took a birthday cake up to his room instead. 'That's really nice,' said Michael, and he came out on to his balcony and shared the cake with members of the adoring public.

By the time we went back to Germany – to Hamburg – Michael and I were getting on better than ever. By this time I, like the rest of the crew, had acquired my own mini fan club – three girls: an Italian, a German and a Spaniard. The Italian was called Claudia, the German was Greta and the Spaniard was Anna. In Hamburg, we'd sometimes take a boat out together for an hour, when I wasn't ensconced in the hotel.

Back at the hotel, I was still taking liberties that other people just wouldn't dare risk. One day I went for a swim but found two of Michael's security men guarding the door to the pool. I realised Michael was in there and turned to go, but the men waved me in. 'It's all right,' said one. 'He knows you.'

I went in. Michael's friend and his family were swimming in the pool, while Michael walked round the edge, wearing a pair of earphones. He lifted a hand in acknowledgement of my presence, after which, on his next circuit of the pool, I pretended I was going to push him in. At first Michael looked a little shocked, but after a moment he found it absolutely hilarious. He was in stitches. He continued his walk, but kept looking at me and making pushing movements. I should think that I was the first person to behave like that with Michael Jackson for very many years.

I must admit, I also played a few jokes. Michael had four adjoining rooms on the first floor of the hotel and I had the fifth (not adjoining.) The fans always discovered which suite Michael was staying in and would wait outside, hoping for a glimpse of him. Occasionally Michael would pull the curtains back and look out, which would prompt a roar of acknowledgement from the crowd. So I bought a pair of white gloves, one of Michael's trademark items of clothing at the time, and I would occasionally twitch my own curtain back, standing well away from the window so that only my hands could be seen. The fans didn't know that the last room wasn't Michael's, and so I too got my own roar of acknowledgement – even if it was actually meant for someone else.

The 'Dangerous' tour occasionally lived up to its name, particularly in Romania. Michael flew in to Bucharest, but three of us were required to drive the three main cars across country to meet him there. We were told to make sure the cars were full of bags of crisps, bottles of water, Coke and so on, because whenever a car stopped, it would be immediately surrounded by the locals. This turned out to be absolutely true. At one point I stopped at a garage (which turned out to have no petrol) and people appeared literally out of nowhere. They were swarming round the car and only went away after I'd thrown packets of peanuts out of the window. The same thing happened when I stopped at a railway junction – I'd had to stop as there were no gates, no lights and no indication as to whether a train was coming or not.

The next problem was petrol: there wasn't any. The other two drivers and I found every garage we stopped at was empty and the three of us somehow coasted in to Bucharest running on empty. There we found that petrol stations attracted the most enormous queues in which you had to wait, literally, for hours. It is common practice in Bucharest to hire someone for the day to queue for you, which means that you could go off and do a full day's work and come back to find that your car, hopefully, is ready.

Because we were with Michael, the police escorted us to the front of the queue, which didn't go down too well with the locals, and a little girl came to fill my car up. She looked so sweet that I handed her a signed picture of Michael. Her little face completely lit up as she looked at the picture: it was as if I'd given her a bag full of gold. After a moment, she handed it back. 'No, no,' I said, 'it's for you.' She looked at me quite wonderingly and carefully stashed the picture away.

Michael was staying at Snagov Lake Palace, the summer residence of President Nicolae Ceausescu before he was killed in 1989. Ceausescu might have fallen but a state of lawlessness remained: there were two buildings in the palace compound and we were told to drive between them rather than walk between them. We were also told not to go in to the grounds after dark. The place was overrun with armed guards – actually teenage boys waving machine guns – and there was a real fear that one might suddenly get trigger happy.

It was a strange set-up. The next day I asked the head of security where I could wash my car: 'Come with me,' he answered. He took me to a compound filled with scruffy young men who, I realised after a moment, were army convicts. They cleaned the car for me, but in the course of doing so, I had to open the boot for them. It was filled with water, Pepsi, crisps, peanuts … The look on their faces was one of absolute amazement to see such abundance inside the car and I felt so sorry for them that I didn't try to stop them when a few cans and packets rapidly vanished.

Michael's enormous humanity was most obviously on display when he made a $1 million donation to a Romanian orphanage called Orphanage Number One. The plight of Romanian orphans, many of whom had either been abandoned or were HIV positive, had been in the news a great deal recently. Michael had been extremely distressed when he had seen pictures of the suffering, and so he decided to make a donation as a way to help.

The day before his visit, I went to see the orphanage and was met on the steps by Richard Young, a well-known paparazzo. A six-year-old boy had latched on to him and was carrying his bags around, while around us, workmen were whitewashing the walls in readiness for Michael's visit. 'Come on, I'll show you around,' Richard said to me.

'I'm not too sure I can take it,' I told him.

'We won't go to the bad bits,' Richard assured me and so we went in. It was very distressing. In a room with thirty or forty cots, the first thing you noticed was the absolute silence. Even when you spoke directly to the babies and tried to amuse them, they would merely stare at you with blank eyes. I couldn't take it after a short time and was forced to leave.

The next day it was time for Michael's visit. The palace was about a thirty-minute journey outside Bucharest, but we had no trouble to begin with: we had twenty or thirty police motorbikes escorting us and at least ten cars. All the junctions had been blocked off in readiness. We roared in to the city to cheering crowds with a highly excited Michael in the back, but as we got close to the orphanage the crowds were so great that the car was forced to slow down to a snail's pace. A couple of the policemen were then knocked off their bikes; they promptly whirled round and started beating the crowd with truncheons.

'Why are they doing that?' asked Michael, unable to believe his eyes.

'They need to clear the road,' I replied.

'But there's no need to do that,' he insisted. He was by now angry and upset and if there had been any way of him getting out of the car and putting a stop to the violence, I am absolutely sure he would have done. We later learned that the crowd was about 40,000 strong.

Once inside the orphanage Michael spent a couple of hours looking around and although very moved by the suffering he saw there, he was very pleased that he was able to make the donation. He later told me that he hadn't realised what an enormous gesture this would seem to the Romanian people, who, I believe, talk about it to this day.

And then, of course, there were the concerts. Capacity was supposed to be 60,000 but there must have been twice as many people as that present. Michael put on his usual brilliant show, but what stood out for me was the backstage catering arrangements. All the food was kept in cages – and standing over it was an armed guard.

On our final day, something very special happened. Michael's people arranged for several hundred soldiers and policemen to gather in a park inside the town. Then Michael arrived. The troops, some on horseback, started marching with Michael at their head: after a minute Michael broke in to a run as the troops marched on, completely straight faced. And so for the next couple of hours Michael walked, talked, ran and danced around the marching troops in one of the most enjoyable sessions I have ever seen on a tour. The day was made for me when he danced past where I was standing and gave me a little wave.

Michael was extremely generous to everyone on the tour, and there were over one hundred of us. In Munich there's a large theme park called Europa Park and Michael booked it one evening for the whole party. He and his friend came along too; the theme was Western style, with a saloon bar and ranches, and they went on all the rides along with the rest of us. Characters from Disneyland wandered amongst us, talking to us and making a fuss of Michael.

Michael always made sure everyone was very well looked after. Although he didn't eat when he was there, dinner was laid out for all of the rest of us. He would sometimes mingle with us in other places, as well, as long as he was sure he wouldn't be mobbed. In Germany we once stayed in a large house rather than a hotel, which was memorable because it featured a miniature bowling alley. Because we were the only people staying there, Michael felt able to come down to the bar and say hello to everyone, although unlike the rest of us, he didn't partake of the famous and delicious German beer.

Michael was far more tolerant of our normal human frailties than most people would have been. In Scotland, he stayed in a house, while we stayed in a hotel about a mile away – a hotel that proved to be totally inadequate. We asked if we could move to another hotel and Michael agreed. While the move was taking place, we were asked to the house in which Michael was staying, where food and drink were laid out for us, along with playing cards and other entertainments. The drink flowed rapidly, with the result that when a call came from Michael's room at about 10 p.m. saying that he wanted one of us to go out and collect some Kentucky Fried Chicken, not one of us was in a fit state to do so. 'Look at you lot,' said an aide. 'You're his drivers and none of you are capable of driving.' Michael took the whole episode in very good heart, though, and sanctioned a mini cab to go out for his late-night snack.

Before the start of every concert, Michael would have an audience with the local children. He was very friendly to them: he'd answer questions, sign autographs and pose for photographs with his young fans. The children absolutely loved it – they were as excited as anyone else about meeting Michael Jackson. When we returned to London, my children – Michael, five, and four-year-old Sheryl – were invited to the meeting and were wildly excited at the prospect.

In the event, the concert was cancelled because Michael had a sore throat, with the result that his audience with the children was cancelled, too. My children were bitterly disappointed but understood that these things do happen. Another member of the crew, however, found out that my kids had been desperate to meet him and were dreadfully upset to have missed out. I didn't know that Michael knew anything about it until he came up to me one day with two signed pictures of himself. 'I know this doesn't compensate for the meeting being cancelled, but at least it's something,' he said, as he handed them over. I looked at the photographs and on them he'd written 'To Michael, love Michael Jackson,' and 'To Sheryl, love Michael Jackson.' I was

particularly touched by this, as Michael usually just puts
'Michael Jackson' on his photographs – and only very rarely
a personal message.

When he was travelling longer distances, Michael would
usually go by plane or on the Orient Express, depending
which one he felt like taking, while the rest of us would drive
our cars to each new destination. This happened towards the
end of my leg of the tour when Michael was performing in
Istanbul when sadly I was never able to say goodbye.

Michael was going to be flying in to the city, while I drove
a Mercedes behind his customised minibus through Turkey,
and it was while I was on my way to the country's capital
that I had the first indication that Turkey wasn't going to be
like the other countries we'd driven through. A car came up
behind me and carved up both me and the minibus, so I
chased him down the road to show he couldn't get away
with that kind of behaviour. Suddenly the car stopped and a
man jumped out: I did likewise to have a word with him. Just
as suddenly, the man pulled a gun on me. I got back in to the
van and it was the last time I gave chase to any car in Turkey.

Once we got to Istanbul we all met up with Michael and
settled down in to the hotel, where we lived in our usual
luxury: food set out for us at all times, beautiful rooms and
so on. However, Michael wasn't at all well and after much
deliberation, it was decided he shouldn't do the show, but

return to London to recuperate instead. I drove him to the airport and had some trouble with the police en route: one car tried to force me off the road, assuming, no doubt, that it would be a great coup to cause trouble for Michael Jackson, while others were cutting me up. It was a nasty experience: my windscreen was smashed and it was with some relief that I got Michael to the plane. Michael never says very much on these occasions, but he was plainly relieved to be leaving.

Initially the concerts were merely postponed until Michael felt better and it wasn't common knowledge that he'd actually left the country. After a couple of days, though, it became apparent that Michael still wasn't better and the concerts were to be cancelled all together. This presented us with a problem. Turkey is a beautiful country but, as I had already discovered, life is rougher there than it is in Western Europe. I wasn't the only one to make this discovery and so there was concern about how the promoters would react when they discovered that Michael had gone and wasn't coming back.

Ultimately and, I believe, wisely, we decided that discretion was the better part of valour and that it would be best for us all to leave before the official announcement was made. Michael's party started trickling out of the hotel in dribs and drabs and we ferried people in relays to the airport. After that was done, we had to get ourselves and the cars out of the country and so we ended up racing through Turkey in three blacked-out Mercedes. It was lucky they were good cars, because the police tried to stop us on a number of occasions, and in each case we got away simply by outspeeding them.

We were still nervous even after crossing the border in to Greece but by the time we made it back to Western Europe our nerves were gone and life returned to normal. Shortly after that I was reunited with my family and the four and a half months I spent on the road with Michael seemed like just a dream.

In the course of those months, Michael did forty-one concerts and I saw every single one of them. The openings were the most amazing stagecraft I have ever seen – and I've seen just about everyone. There would be a dramatic burst of music, which would build up in intensity along with flashbacks of Michael throughout the years. Then the lights would go down, the music would become increasingly frenzied and the stage would suddenly explode in fireworks as Michael himself exploded out of the floor from a 'toaster', something that made headlines all over the world. The crowd would go absolutely wild. Michael would stand absolutely still for as much as a minute – and it takes an inordinate amount of charisma to be able to stand on stage alone holding a crowd of thousands – then he would suddenly turn and hold his pose for another minute as the crowds erupted again. At the end of the concerts, he would leave wearing a jet pack – another world first.

And so that was my time with Michael Jackson: a musical genius, a truly kind and nice man and, for a very short time, a friend. I'm so glad for him that he has children of his own now and I wish him nothing but happiness in the future. And as for his music and his performances, I can only quote what someone else said in a very different context – baby, you're the best.

\* \* \* \* \*

I met a couple of other members of the family over the years and to be honest, they aren't a patch on Michael. The first was Latoya, his younger sister, whom I met off Concorde with her then husband and manager, Jack Gordon. Of course, I recognised Latoya immediately and even if I hadn't, it would have been obvious she was a star. Latoya absolutely loves the attention she gets and was playing the crowds for all she was worth: fluttering her eyelashes, wiggling around, putting on and taking off sunglasses and generally acting the star. Jack was struggling behind her with the suitcases so I went over to him: 'Mr Gordon,' I said, 'let me help.'

It immediately turned out that I had made a mistake in

Jack Gordon's book in talking to him without holding up a name board, as is the usual practice. He looked at me in a wary manner. 'Have we met before?' he said in a tone that could easily have served as an ice pick.

'No sir, we haven't. But since you're standing right behind a member of the Jackson family, whom I recognised as I have seen approximately 18,243 pictures of her in the newspapers and I knew she was married to her manager and that that manager was called Jack Gordon, it's a fairly obvious assumption that you would be he. And I was correct, was I not? You are that Jack Gordon? And you are accompanying Latoya Jackson, who has an even more famous brother called Michael with whom I recently spent a few months and who has more courtesy in his little fingernail than you have just shown? Now I will drive you in to London, as I am being paid to do. And might I add that your wife is wearing far too much make-up.'

Actually, I said nothing of the sort. I just picked up their bags and got on with it. But I certainly thought it.

I also met Germaine Jackson – extremely briefly – when I was called to meet him and his family at the Conrad Hotel in Chelsea. Germaine came across as a decent man, and polite with it. He and his family had just been eating and offered me a sandwich, which I gratefully accepted as you can go for hours and sometimes even days without eating in this job.

The family then went to their rooms to change, while I want to wait outside. And so I waited. And waited. And waited ... Finally, over two hours later, a minion appeared. 'Sorry about this,' he said, 'but they've decided not to go out after all.'

'Couldn't someone have told me?'

'They, er, forgot you were here,' said the minion and went back inside. *Oh well*, I thought, *thanks for the sandwich ...*

# Do Ya Think
# I'm Sexy?

ROD STEWART WANTED a new Bentley. He had one already, but it was black, it was old and he wanted something new. So it was no surprise when I went to pick him up one day, ostensibly for a shopping trip in London, that Rod had other things on his mind. 'We're gonna have to wait a while, Keith,' he told me, with all the keen anticipation of a child about to receive his first bicycle. 'Something's on its way.' Half an hour later something – or rather, two somethings – appeared in the driveway sweeping up to the house. Two brand new P-reg Bentleys, one maroon and one green. 'Yes!' said Rod. 'Which one do you think I should buy, Keith?'

I walked over and had a look around both of them. 'I like the green one, Rod,' I said.

'I fancy the maroon,' said Rod. He opened the door of the maroon Bentley and slid in. 'Great stuff,' he announced. But then he changed his mind almost immediately when he opened the door of the green car and the steering wheel slid back to allow him room to get in. 'Woah!' he exclaimed. 'The old one didn't do this!' He had a further look around at the incredibly luxurious white leather interior, the sensors on the bumpers, the array of lights that showed you when you were getting too close to the curb … 'I'm having this one! – as long as we can do a deal,' bellowed Rod. 'Take the red one away.'

The deal – part-exchange of the old Bentley – done, I went off to collect the tax disk and insurance papers and returned to find Rod crooning over his new baby. 'It's much better than the old one,' he announced, stroking the exterior. 'What do you think, Keith? Don't you think it's better?' It certainly had a lot more gadgets than the old one and Rod was beside himself with joy.

We couldn't drive it straight away, though, because Rod had to have the windows blacked out. This is essential for a celebrity of Rod's stature: if a car like his gets stuck in traffic and people can see who's inside, you can end up getting a lot of aggro. The only car windows Rod doesn't have blacked out are those on his sports cars: otherwise his limos, like Mick's and those of my other famous clients, are all protected from the public gaze.

Which is just as well, given what Rod got up to when we took the car out for a trial run a couple of days later. We went up to London to make that delayed shopping trip with Rod and his great friend Alan Sewell in the back. Alan is a scrap metal merchant who also lives in Epping and is one of Rod's closest friends, while his wife Debbie used to be friends with Rod's ex-wife Rachel. (Amongst other entertainments, they used to hold farting competitions in the back of the car, to see who could produce the loudest and longest explosion.) I took a short cut past Horseguard's Parade before turning on to the Mall. Horseguard's Parade is in Whitehall, behind the War Office and it is strictly forbidden to drive on to it. To reinforce the point, there is a very high curb and a chain fence to keep people away. 'Is that Horseguard's Parade?' asked Rod.

'Yes.'

'Can we drive on to it?'

'No. It's prohibited.'

'Keith,' said Rod, 'I bet you £2,000 you won't drive on to it.'

'I can't afford to lose that kind of money,' I replied.

'Okay,' said Rod, 'I'll pay you two grand in cash if you drive on to it now.'

'Rod,' I said, 'have you any idea what would happen if your car was found to be driving on Horseguard's Parade?'

'Fuck, there are chains out there,' said Rod, not paying any attention. 'Alan, can you get out and try and undo the chains?'

Alan got out, found he couldn't undo the chains. Then he found one chain-free part of the Parade – but the curb there was a foot high.

'Do it!' urged Rod.

'No!'

'Do it!'

'No!'

'Chicken,' sniffed Rod and, rather gloomily, Alan got back in to the car.

I had a good reason to be cautious, though – or rather, two. First, it would have damaged the car and however cool Rod might have been about it at the time, I had no doubt that he'd go ballistic afterwards should his car have come to any harm. Secondly, a black BMW kept reappearing as we drove around and sure enough, it appeared again as we drove off. We parked at the Mayfair Hotel and as Rod opened the door to get out, two paparazzi – Dave Bennett and Richard Young

– leapt out and started taking pictures. 'What were you doing at Horseguard's Parade?' one of them yelled.

'Ask Keith!' grinned Rod before disappearing inside.

There was no harm now, so I told them the truth. Their faces dropped like children being deprived of candy. 'Oh I wish you had,' said Richard. 'The pictures we could have taken,' sighed Dave. 'We wouldn't have had to work for a month.'

That wasn't the only time Rod and Alan behaved badly together, either. Once when I picked them up after a concert at Wembley, Rod urgently needed the loo but equally urgently wanted to get home. The back of the car was filled with bottles of wine, water, Pepsi and paper cups. It was this last that Rod noticed. 'Let me use that,' he said.

Alan joined in the fun. 'See how many you can fill, Rod!' he began and so Rod spent the rest of the journey urinating in to paper cups and then tossing them out of the car. One, I regret to say, hit another chauffeur.

\* \* \* \* \*

It was 1991 when I first went to collect one of my company's most difficult-to-please employees: Rod Stewart. Rod was, and still is, incredibly fussy. He finds fault, and most drivers only lasted one journey. So I was feeling rather nervous about meeting this most pernickety of men.

I turned through the electric gates in to the long drive that leads up to Rod's home in Epping and drew in my breath. Rod might be the world's most famous Essex boy, but it doesn't show in his tastes: I saw before me manicured lawns dotted with statues, beautiful flower beds – Rod has three full-time gardeners – a swimming pool, guest house and the main forecourt of the house on which was parked a white Lamborghini, a red Ferrari and a black Mercedes. There was no doubt that I was in the home of a very successful man.

A deeply tanned Rod came out to meet me wearing stonewashed jeans, a red wool V-neck slipover and a 1960s polka dotted shirt. I'd been a fan of Rod and The Faces for years, so I felt quite humble when he got in to the back of my car – and promptly fell asleep as we drove to Elstree Studios, where he was rehearsing for the 'Vagabond' tour. Eventually, however, he woke up and, noticing the lack of traffic about, asked, 'Are we going to a funeral?' Then he laughed uproariously and settled back in the car. That was the beginning of an association that was to last seven years.

I only began to realise it had gone well that night, though, when we returned to Rod's mansion at about eleven o'clock. 'Look Keith,' said Rod, 'I'm going to need you again at nine in the morning. Why don't you stay in the guest house overnight?'

'But Rod, I don't have a clean shirt and a shave,' I told him.

'You'll find everything you need in the guest house,' he answered. 'Just make yourself at home.' And just as I was doing just that, there was a knock on the door: it was Rod, holding a clean shirt and a pint of milk. 'See you in the morning!' he said.

The guest house, like the main mansion, was beautiful. Carpeted all over in cream shag pile, it had two bedrooms, two bathrooms, a massive wood-fitted kitchen and a television with about fifty channels on it, or so it seemed. The colour scheme was magnolia and the place was dotted about with antiques. I had a very good night's sleep and got up early the next morning to wash the car, when I saw Rod watching me through the window. 'You're eager,' he said.

This was in the early days of Rod's marriage to the stunning New Zealand model Rachel Hunter and though the age difference was later to cause problems – when the couple married in 1991, Rod was forty-five and Rachel twenty-one – at this point they were still deliriously happy. Rod had reportedly chased Rachel from the moment he set eyes on her in a Los Angeles nightclub and when I met Rachel later that day, I could quite see why he had popped the question after just three weeks. She was with her sister Jackie and even dressed in jeans and an old shirt, she looked simply stunning. Rod had just bought her a couple of horses and she was on her way to the stables. She was nice and polite, but in the early days rather reserved. This changed when I drove her to Stansted one day for a modelling assignment.

'Keith,' she gasped as she rifled through her handbag prior to getting out of the car on arrival, 'I've left my passport behind!'

'You go to the VIP lounge,' I advised. 'I'll be back as fast as I can.' I drove off at speed, got back to the house, collected her passport and made it back to the airport in time, which seemed to break the ice between us. From then on, she would ask me about myself and my family and talked a lot about how much she wanted to have children herself. Shortly afterwards she became pregnant with Renee, the daughter who was born in 1992, which bore out Rod's answers when asked what he was up to at the moment. 'Just shagging the missus!' he'd say.

Renee was born in London's Portland Hospital, which is where Jerry Hall, Nicole Appleton, Victoria Beckham and Zoe Ball also gave birth to their children. The place was surrounded by paparazzi and so Rod would be sneaked in via the boot of his car – a popular form of transport for so many of the celebrities I've worked with. He could usually only stand a minute or so, though, before he demanded to be let out. I sneaked both of them out for dinner in Harry's Bar just two days after the birth – although this time we used a side door, as Rachel wasn't quite up to the boot of a car, disguising themselves by piling boxes at the front of the car. A day or two later we went shopping in Chelsea, after which Rod showered her with presents. At that time they couldn't have been more in love.

They both loved children and they were both kind to my son Michael, who was just five at the time. Michael met the Stewarts when I was asked to collect a birdcage from Harrods and deliver it to the house. I took Michael with me and when Rod saw the little boy in the car, he asked if he would like to help collect twigs for the cage. Greatly excited, Michael set off to help his father's famous employer, before trotting back to the house at Rod's invitation. Once there, Rod poured him a glass of lemonade in one of his heavy crystal tumblers.

'Er, Rod,' I began, terrified that Michael would drop the beautiful glass, 'he's only young –'

'It's all right,' said Rod affably and Michael was allowed to gulp away from the valuable crystal.

The couple were also really nice to us a few months later, when I took Michael and my then girlfriend, Jill, to see one of Rod's concerts. Rod had given us tickets for the Royal Box and invited us to see him backstage halfway through the show. When we got there and found Rachel waiting for us, Michael promptly burst in to tears. 'What's wrong Michael?' asked Rachel, scooping him up in her arms.

'We're sitting so far away I can't see,' sobbed Michael.

'Well, why don't you stay here backstage?' suggested Rachel. Michael agreed and she took him to the edge of the stage. Rod kicks footballs out in to the audience in the course of his act and Rachel suggested Michael carry them out on stage; the little boy was too shy, though, in front of such a huge audience, and so he threw the footballs from the wings, instead.

Apart from women – and during his marriage to Rachel he gave up all other women – Rod's two great loves are cars and football. During the time I was with him, Rod had innumerable cars and when he was away in LA, where he has his other main home, he would ask me to go up to Epping and take the cars for a drive – something that I was only too happy to do. He already had a white Lamborghini Countach and to this he added a red Lamborghini Diablo. 'Come on, let's take them both out,' he said one day. 'I'll take the red one, you take the white.'

'But Rod, why do you want me to drive separately?' I asked.

'I want to see how the white one moves,' Rod replied, tossing me the key. And so we set off for a factory estate in Hatfield, where Rod had heard of an AC Cobra he wanted to see. When we drew up it caused a sensation: one of these space ships is more than enough to draw a crowd and two created uproar, especially when Rod got out. Rod loved the attention; he signed autographs and chatted away – before deciding he wasn't going to buy the new car after all.

Rod did end up with a Cobra, but in a round-about way. He attended a charity lunch at the Inn on the Park where he and Sir Elton John vied for two items in the charity auction: an AC Cobra replica and a gold microphone. Rod got the first, Sir Elt the second and they both paid around £25,000 for their choices. A couple of hours later, I had to drive Rod and Rachel to a modelling shoot, after which I was sent back to collect the car.

It was still in the middle of the room in which the auction was raised and had to be lifted out with a forklift truck before I was able to take it to Rod's house. It sat on the forecourt for about a week until Rod finally had a spin in it, after which he decided that he didn't like it after all because he wanted the real thing, not a replica. He thus finally bought an AC Cobra, which was bright yellow with a green stripe – and a snip at £140,000.

Sir Elton was responsible for one of the more memorable moments in one of Rod's concerts. Rod was playing Wembley and in the course of the show, a French waiter would appear on stage with a glass of wine, which he would give to Rod before disappearing. Rod would then sit on a sofa and sip the wine before launching in to the next song.

One evening, a woman in full evening dress appeared on

the stage with the glass of wine. Rod hadn't been told of any change in plan, and so he was a little taken aback as the woman glided across the stage and presented him with his wine. Surprise turned to consternation, though, as not only did the woman not disappear – she actually sat down on Rod's lap.

The band fell silent and the audience began to whisper until suddenly Rod started howling with laughter. Then the band joined in and finally the audience as they began to realise that the elegantly dressed woman was in fact Sir Elton, camping it up in full drag. She, or rather he, stood up, blew kisses to everyone and then left as abruptly as she'd arrived while Rod got on with the show. The next day a big bouquet of flowers arrived at Rod's house with a card attached that read, 'Thanks for letting me sit on your lap last night. Love, Sharon.'

Rod is a trouper of the old school when it comes to performing: he takes it very seriously. One night he was due to perform in Sheffield but he was suffering from a sore throat, which was getting steadily worse. His doctor, Dr David Forecast, who has treated many celebrities, wanted him to cancel his performance, but Rod was insistent that the show should go on. Then he started coughing up blood. 'Rod, you've got to cancel,' Dr Forecast insisted.

'Just give me something to get on stage,' Rod replied.

Dosed up to the nines with painkillers, Rod was driven up to Sheffield, with Dr Forecast in attendance. I was sitting backstage and could hear him all too clearly. The man sounded terrible, but he was determined not to let his fans down. Somehow he got through the performance, although he had to keep coming off stage to give his voice a rest. 'Rod, I'm getting seriously worried,' said Dr Forecast at one point. 'After the show, I think you should go to Sheffield hospital.'

'No, I want to get home to Rachel,' was Rod's response.

We had no idea what sort of condition he would be in when he finally came off stage, so we called an ambulance to wait in case he really did have to go to hospital, and decked my car out with drips. He eventually came off stage, adamant that he wanted to go home. So he was given an injection, hooked on to a drip and I drove back as fast as I could. Rod was asleep for most of the journey, but he woke up as we neared the house, very confused. 'I don't feel well,' he muttered. The next day he was in such a bad way that he had to go in to hospital. 'But I did do the concert,' he said triumphantly.

Back then, when Rod and Rachel were happily married, I used to take them to local restaurants and sit at a table nearby or drive them to Rod's local, The Boyden Arms. Rod drinks Caffrey's, a drink much like Guinness, which takes a couple of minutes to settle. It was a two-and-a-half-minute drive from the house to the pub, so just as we were starting out, Rod would ring the landlord and get him to pull a pint so it would be ready just as he came in.

Rod was a regular and treated as such by everyone except for one Rod Stewart lookalike, who came in so often and pestered the original so much that he had to be thrown out. 'Exactly how many autographs does he need?' Rod asked in exasperation. Usually Rod would stand with the lads and talk about football and if Rachel was with him, she'd be treated normally, too. It's simply not true that Rod never buys a round, incidentally – I have seen him do so on numerous occasions.

Back then, Rod and Rachel were head over heels in love and it showed. On one occasion in 1994, shortly after the birth of their son Liam, I drove the two of them to Birmingham, where Rod was doing a concert at the National Exhibition Centre. They came out of the house looking like young lovers: they were giggling away, kissing and cuddling and generally acting up. We got in to the Daimler. The kissing and cuddling went on. By the time we reached the motorway, the partition had gone up. The kissing and cuddling continued and then Rod produced a notebook, scribbled something and handed it to Rachel. 'Oh darling, that's nice,' she said. (I could still hear them, despite the partition.)

She scribbled something back. 'Lovely,' said Rod and passed another note to her.

'Oh no, not that!' squawked Rachel and handed another note back. Rod giggled lecherously and handed another one back. This went on for some time, with Rachel becoming increasingly shocked at the notes Rod was giving her, with a lot more giggling and joking, until they finally reached their journey's end.

After they'd got out, I found one of the notes Rod had written Rachel in the back of the car. It said:

1 – When the car gets going, get your tits out

2 – Cig's stuck up asshole and you will suck it up.

Theirs never was the most sophisticated of relationships.

\* \* \* \* \*

The press loved them and Rod and Rachel reacted in different ways. On one occasion a picture was taken of the couple sunbathing, when Rachel was wearing just a G-string, which made much of Rachel's charming bottom, and published in a tabloid newspaper. Rod was extremely annoyed, whereas Rachel thought it was funny. The next day when I drove them with Don, Rod's PR man, to Stansted, an airline official came out to check how many people were flying. 'Three?' he asked. 'Oh no,' said Rachel, 'just two and a bum.'

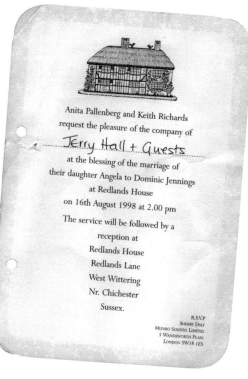

Anita Pallenberg and Keith Richards
request the pleasure of the company of

*Jerry Hall + Guests*

at the blessing of the marriage of
their daughter Angela to Dominic Jennings
at Redlands House
on 16th August 1998 at 2.00 pm

The service will be followed by a
reception at

Redlands House
Redlands Lane
West Wittering
Nr. Chichester
Sussex.

R.S.V.P
SHERRY DALY
MUNRO SOUNDS LIMITED
5 WANDSWORTH PLAIN
LONDON SW18 1ES

*Top*: Driving Mick and Jerry.

*Bottom left*: Escorting Mick to an exclusive celebrity party in London's Knightsbridge.

*Bottom right*: An invitation Keith Richards and Anita Pallenberg sent to Jerry for the wedding of their daughter.

This signed picture of Rod shows him at his most charming. But the note (*inset*) he left in the back of the car shows a rather different side to Mr Stewart…

Michael Jackson – one of the nicest men I have ever known. (*Inset*) My backstage pass for Michael's *Dangerous* tour.

Ol' Blue Eyes wrote this kind note for me after I escorted him in 1990.

For Keith —
many thanks for all
your help in showing
the girls your Marvelou
City! All the Best to Yo
Frank Sinatra
July '90

*Top*: A signed photo from Gloria Estefan.

*Bottom*: Barbra Streisand and her entourage. That's me on Barbra's right.

To
Keith,
Thank you for Everything,
your friend,
Celine
Dion
xo...

Celine Dion – one of the many 'pretty women' it's been my pleasure to drive.

've driven so many stars from both sides of the Atlantic. A few of them are pictured
ere: Jack Lemmon (*top left*), Paul Young (*top right*), Steven Seagal (*bottom left*) and
he beautiful Mariah Carey (*bottom right*).

REBECCA DE MORNAY

Keith —
Just wanted to say how much your thoughtful manner and consummate professionalism was appreciated. You made the hectic London leg of the tour that much more pleasant.
Thank you. And all the best

Rebecca

*Top:* Rebecca De Mornay wrote me this note to say how much she appreciated my services.

*Bottom:* Me in the office!

Rod did have a temper though, and on occasion he took it out on me. When Rod played Manchester, I'd take him to Stansted by private jet and another of our drivers would take a car up and meet him there. One year I was coincidentally going to be in Manchester, so I asked him if I could take my son to see one of his concerts. 'Fine,' he said. 'It'll be company for Liam.'

When I actually got there, though, it was obvious that he had completely forgotten all about our conversation. I collected him from the airport and noticed he was unusually quiet. Suddenly he erupted. 'What are you doing here?' he shouted. 'Who's paying for you to come up here? This is a complete waste of money.'

I kept trying to remind him of our conversation and tell him we always sent a driver up here, but Rod was having none of it. He continued to shout until we got to the hotel, after which he stormed out, ignoring my son who had come out to greet us, and went in to the hotel shouting. I was so angry about his behaviour – as, incidentally, was my son – that I was all for turning back on the spot and going home. When Rod had calmed down, though, he sent his long term PA Don Archell out to calm me down in turn and later came out to apologise in person.

On another occasion, Rod and Rachel were coming back

from Birmingham in my company's Daimler. Rod pulled the screen down: 'It's really cold back here,' he said.

'The controls are on the side of the seat. Don't turn them too far or the heat will go off,' I replied.

The screen went back up again: a few minutes later it came down. Rod still hadn't worked out how to use the controls and no, he didn't want me to get in the back of the car to show him how. This happened three or four times until Rod started shouting, 'I'm not going to pay for this car. It's cold. I'm not paying for this, what do you think you're doing, sending me a car like this –'

I pulled over, got in the back of the car, turned the heat on, regained my seat and drove off. The screen went up again and I didn't hear a peep for the rest of the journey.

Rod has a reputation for being careful with his money and it's deserved, as I discovered on one occasion that really surprised me. I had taken Rod and Rachel Christmas shopping in London, when Rod suddenly said to me, 'We've got to get gifts for your kids, too Keith.'

'That's very good of you, Rod,' I said.

Rod gave me several thousand US dollars to change in to sterling while he and Rachel went off for lunch and then the three of us went on to Harrods to get presents for everyone, including my kids. We couldn't park anywhere though, so I said, 'We can leave it for now, Rod. I'll drive round, come back to collect you and we can get gifts another time.'

Rod went off with Rachel, but when he got back, he gave me a fist full of notes. 'Here,' he said. 'That's to get something for your kids.' I looked at it later and was quite overwhelmed. Rod had given me £400 – and Rod never gives anyone Christmas boxes. Never.

He hadn't given me one, either, as I belatedly discovered the next day. I was called up early and asked to pick up some stuff for Rachel, which came to £147. Then I got to the house. 'How much do you owe me?' asked Rod.

'Eh?'

'The money I gave you yesterday. What's left after you got Rachel's stuff?'

'But Rod,' I said, 'I spent £200 on gifts for my kids. And then Rachel's stuff came to £147 ...'

'Than that's £53,' said Rod calmly. 'Can I have it, mate?' And he even waited until I'd dug up £3 in coins. Rod Stewart, incidentally, is not a poor man.

Rod's other great passion, as I said before, is football. He has his own football grounds and his own team at home in Epping and when Scotland were playing, he'd take the whole pub crowd up to see the match in a private jet. He always attends the FA Cup and one year went to a replay of the FA Cup with Ronnie Woods, the late comedian Peter Cook and Jimmy Wyatt, the snooker player. Rod instructed everyone that it was essential they be back in the car five minutes before the game ended: needless to say, poor old Peter Cook, who was in the advanced stages of alcoholism at the time, did not make it to the car. 'Well, we did tell him,' commented Rod. 'Let's go.' We drove off and two and a half hours later Peter found us in a pub in Hampstead, barely able to stand up, let alone able tell us how he'd got there.

Rod and Rachel loved animals. Some years ago, they decided to buy two Alsatians to train as guard dogs. I was driving a Mercedes that was two days old and so covered the seats with newspapers and blankets to make sure the dogs did nothing to destroy it, before taking them to kennels near Guildford. We found nothing that day and eventually left to take Rod to his record company in Kensington.

The next day I took Rachel up to some kennels near Reading where she found two puppies to her liking and after dropping them off, I was relieved to see the two dogs had behaved themselves perfectly and the blankets were dry. When I took the newspaper up, however, I found the newsprint had imprinted itself on the seat of the car … At least the dogs were professionally trained, though, and as far as I know, are guard dogs at Epping to this day.

Rod was in Los Angeles when his much-loved mother Elsie died in 1998. He was devastated. Rod was very close to his mother, who lived in Muswell Hill, North London, and so he was in a sombre mood when I picked him up from the airport to attend the funeral. We drove back to his house and, with a couple of hours to go before we set off, I went for a walk around the grounds. It was a blisteringly hot day but, ever the professional, I kept my jacket on, my tie correctly tied and donned a pair of sunglasses. Because of the heat, though, I sat down next to the pool to be near the cool water and was startled when I realised Rod was taking pictures of me: 'You look like a member of the Mafia,' he explained.

The funeral was in Muswell Hill, after which there was a reception at the British Legion, an old favourite of his parents – and Rod is still a member himself. After that Rod invited everyone first to a restaurant and then back to The Boydon Arms where, despite he became very emotional about the fact that the family was all together. 'Come on, let's have a good old drink to see her off,' he said. After a while, Rod started singing and dancing, tapping out tunes on the hanging brasswork with sticks he carries with him. 'It's what she would have wanted, Keith,' he told me.

\* \* \* \* \*

Rod wasn't over-fond of Mick Jagger. Whenever I was unable to drive him because I was taking Mick around, Rod would say, 'You've been out with that MJ bloke, haven't you?' Whether this is rivalry I don't know, but it might go back a long way – to when Ronnie Wood joined the Stones from Rod's band The Faces, perhaps. 'You know, Jagger always said to me: "I'd never steal Woody from you Rod." Well of course he DID!'

I was with Mick full time for some time after that and so I wasn't aware that something was going seriously wrong in Rod's relationship with Rachel. The first hint I had was when the two of them were pictured outside a restaurant in Chelsea. Rachel was screaming at Rod and Rod was cowering like a little boy. One of my drivers had been taking them out that night, so the next day I rang him. 'What on earth was that all about?' I asked.

The driver sighed. 'They were screaming at each other in the restaurant and the row went on outside,' he replied. 'When they got in to the car, you could have broken the atmosphere with a pick axe. They didn't say a word all the way home and when we got back to Epping, they just stormed off in silence.'

Shortly after that I went to pick Rod up after a concert. About half an hour from the start of the show, while I was waiting to see if Rod wanted to hang around or do a runner, I suddenly realised that Rachel wasn't there. I phoned the driver who was supposed to be collecting her. 'Where is she?' I demanded. 'Rod's about to come off stage and you know what he'll be like if she's not there.'

'She's still in her suite at The Dorchester,' the driver replied. 'She's refusing to come down. What can I do, Keith, I can hardly go in there and drag her out, can I?'

Rachel didn't turn up that night, which was very unusual for her and after a couple of drinks, Rod went home alone. Two days later I had to send a car to their home to pick up Rachel and the children. She took them to LA and a couple of days later it was officially announced they had parted.

It was 1998 and the couple have been separated since then. It was the first time a woman left Rod rather than the other way around, and he changed a lot after that. For a start, he was gutted – he really did love Rachel. Then he became increasingly irritable and very depressed. He was drinking a lot and making snide comments all the time. He also began losing his temper with other people and for a time was very difficult with other people.

Rachel Hunter later said that she spent sleepless nights plotting her escape from Rod, because she couldn't continue 'living a lie' as his devoted wife. 'To the outside world, I was mother of two beautiful kids, a wife to Rod and a successful model without any financial worries, but, inside, I was in torment,' she revealed. 'By the time I was twenty-nine, I had spent eight years with someone else's group of friends.

'In the nine years we were together, I'd never done anything for myself. If you'd asked me then what I liked or didn't like, I wouldn't have been able to tell you. I didn't even have a hobby. Like lots of women who marry young and find themselves mothers by the time they're twenty-five, I felt I no longer had an identity. I was just nothing.

'I'd become so cosseted, I was too scared to do anything for myself. Last year, I took the amazing step of travelling from Los Angeles to London entirely on my own and spent a week just meeting people and making my own friends.'

Rachel went on to say that Rod was 'a great dad and a good lover' and the love of her life. The relationship was 'fiery and tempestuous and it was always fun,' she said 'When he used to say all those things about "shaggin' the missus", I really didn't mind. I loved his sense of humour. He's living proof that a man can laugh you into bed.' And Rachel recalled that when they got engaged, 'He took me for a picnic to a lovely park in Los Angeles and got down on one knee to ask me to be his wife … At first, I went into complete shock. But I had no hesitation in saying, "Yes." He presented me with a beautiful diamond and sapphire ring from Van Cleef.'

But the age difference was beginning to show. Rod enjoyed going to the pub with his friends or staying at home playing with his train set, while Rachel, a young woman, wanted to go out and party. 'You don't understand when you're twenty-one and in love that to progress, you need to grow with your partner,' she said. 'We didn't. I soon realized there was a certain difference in attitudes. You can't really expect a twenty-two-year-old girl to react the same way as a man twenty-four years older than her.'

Rachel revealed that she finally realized she needed to leave one day, during a grocery run. At the supermarket, she saw an old woman shuffling down the aisle with her shopping basket and realized that could one day be her. 'I can remember thinking: Here I am, approaching thirty and Oh, shit, what am I doing with my life?' she said. 'I knew very definitely in that instant that I didn't want to get to that age and have any regrets about what I've done or not done. It gave me the impetus to move on.'

Rod took it very badly. 'He was distraught,' admitted Rachel. 'I'll take to the grave the pain that I caused Rod. I hurt the one person I loved and cared about, and that's a hard thing to live with on a daily basis.' But Rachel admitted that she felt happier with a simple life in California. 'I left with the only things I wanted – some precious memories, a few photographs of Rod and I with Renee and Liam, and my wedding ring,' she said. 'Looking back, it might have been better if we had argued more often. At least that way there'd have been some communication. There are people who say I was selfish to break up the family, but I knew that to go on living a lie was a less healthy option for all of us.

'It's been a long healing process,' she admitted. 'There were moments when I'd be walking along the beach or out riding when sadness would come over me in waves. You can't walk away from nine years of your life and expect to feel nothing. For someone who has always been in a relationship, it's strange.'

To be honest, I think she might regret it. Rod might be a lot older than her but they had some very good times together, to say nothing of two children. But they are about to get divorced. It's a shame.

# Je Suis Un
# Rock Star

THE YEAR 1993 was a busy one for Bill Wyman. He kicked off by quitting the Stones, went on to get married for the third time and then saw his thirty-year-old son Stephen announce that he was to marry forty-six-year-old Patsy Smith, the mother of Bill's teen bride Mandy Smith. This union – which never took place – would have made Bill the father-in-law of his former mother-in-law, and the step-grandfather of his former wife, which is a lot for any man to take on board. Bill himself remains wryly amused by his own complicated and tangled love life. It's not a subject that comes up for discussion that often – but Bill is able to laugh at his own expense. Sometimes.

Actually, as it turned out, that year was to be the making of Bill. He finally settled down with the right woman, became a family man, gave up the womanising that could have landed him not only in trouble but in jail and even established himself as a pillar of the community, with houses in Chelsea, Suffolk and the South of France. Like Mick, he's gone from rock rebel to rock aristocracy and has become a pillar of the establishment in the process. And unlike Mick, he's had the sense to give up other women, now that he's a happily married man. And not before time, too. Unbelievably, after turning sixty-five in 2001, Bill Wyman is now officially an old age pensioner and eligible for a bus pass.

Despite my long association with the Stones, I had never actually met Bill until 1993, although I did occasionally see him in the background. However, after Bill married the thirty-three-year-old American actress Suzanne Accosta in Nice, near his home in the South of France, in the April of that year, he needed someone to drive him on his honeymoon. Thanks to a recommendation from Mick, that someone turned out to be me. After being told not to take any suits with me, as Bill hates being driven by men in suits, I flew out to the South of France at short notice and was taken to Bill's villa in Vence in the South of France.

So yet again I had the experience of finally meeting in the

flesh someone I'd known of for a long time. Bill was exactly as I'd imagined he would be: very cool and laid back. Slightly to my surprise, though, he was absolutely tiny. Suzanne was extremely pretty and lively and an awful lot younger than Bill, although not quite as young as Bill's second wife Mandy, who had been only thirteen when they first met. Suzanne was, at least, a grown woman and one that I initially took to on meeting. We all got on very well that first time and it was only later, sadly, that our relationship turned sour.

After a relaxed lunch, in which we all got to know each other, we loaded the boot of Bill's car with all the paraphernalia they were to take on honeymoon – only to discover that the car wouldn't start. It was an old Mercedes that had belonged to Mick and, in typical rock star style, came complete with a television in the back. The only trouble was that, rock star or no, the television used to drain the batteries, so we were always jump-starting the car. 'I'm getting that thing taken out,' muttered Bill climbing in to the jump started Merc after we finally got it going and with that we all drove off on honeymoon.

It could have been awkward, being a third party with a newly married couple, but it is a mark of how well we all got on that the journey was as pleasant for me as it seemed to be for the happy couple. And I did get to see some beautiful places on the way. The first night was spent in the charming

Italian town of Portofino. Bill and Suzanne behaved like any newlyweds would: giggling, kissing and holding hands as we drove in to the town and vanishing for some considerable time in to their hotel suite before they were ready to re-emerge. I had dinner with them that night as they needed me on hand for security reasons – even on honeymoon, a celebrity as big as Bill Wyman can not be left on his own – and I also accompanied them back to the hotel for a drink. As the night progressed and the two became increasingly amorous, I began to feel more like a gooseberry than a bodyguard. I said as much to Bill.

'A gooseberry?' said Suzanne (she's American and so doesn't pick up on every cultural reference). 'What's that?'

'A third person around a couple,' I told her. 'Now I'm really enjoying your company but there's plenty of security here in the hotel. I don't think you're going to have any problems around here. Wouldn't you prefer it if I went up to my room? You know where I am if you need me.'

'That's fine,' said Bill, so I left the happy couple to coo at one another alone under the stars.

The next morning we set off for Lake Como, where we were to spend three days. Bill is very keen on metal detectors, so after we had settled in to the next hotel, he spent much of the time scouring the shores of the lake looking for treasure. He didn't actually find any, but he seemed happy, nonetheless. It was a lovely time for me. I was on hand when the couple needed to go anywhere or when they needed extra security but apart from that, my time was my own, to wander about the place as I pleased. That's another of the perks of the job: not only do you get to meet a lot of interesting people, but you get to see a lot of lovely places, too.

And from there it was on to Montreux where, to Bill's great satisfaction, he was recognised and asked to sign autographs (your average celebrity may hate being spotted but he hates it a whole lot more when he's not spotted) and finally we spent a couple of days driving through France to Paris. It was then that I got the first intimation as to the mixed feelings Bill had about his old band, the one that had brought him riches and fame, the one known as The Rolling Stones. 'You know, Keith,' he said as we drove through the beautiful French countryside, 'I'm thinking of starting my own band to play the kind of music I really love listening to – blues and jazz from the 1930s.'

'Don't you listen to the Stones?' I asked, astonished that he didn't mention them. Now that I came to think about it, he hadn't once mentioned them since we'd met.

'I don't think so,' he said and that, for a long time, was the end of that. I later discovered that Bill felt miffed. Mick and Keith are the two leading members of the band, with Ronnie

Woods coming up third. Bill and Charlie were never considered to be quite in the same league as the others – Bill saw it like that, at any rate – and were never given the chance to grow musically in the way they wanted to, which is probably why both have their own bands. Charlie, who has a happy life with his own brass band and his wife's stud farm, as I describe elsewhere in the book, never let any of this bother him, but Bill is thin skinned and didn't like it. He continued to be in touch with the other Stones and his wife is a friend of Jerry's, but he's never regretted dropping out of one of the most famous rock and roll bands in the world.

I didn't know any of this back then: I was just enjoying getting to know another Rolling Stone and his wife as well as relishing some time in the country. And it was a lovely week, casual and laid back. You'd never have thought that the Bill Wyman I was driving around France, who spent his time spotting castles and falcons, pointing out buildings of special architectural interest and displaying an extremely impressive knowledge of the local wildlife, was the same Bill Wyman who had caused such an outcry when he romanced the teenage Mandy Smith and who claimed to have slept with, literally, thousands of women in the heyday of The Rolling Stones. It was said that he used to pick girls out through his hotel window and get his minder to invite them to his room; on occasion, Bill would entertain a number of girls in one afternoon. But this Bill, new Bill, was quiet and happily married, nothing like the hell-raiser I had heard so much about in the past.

Despite the fact that we'd all enjoyed one another's company, though, our parting was very abrupt. I delivered the happy couple to the hotel in which they were staying in Paris in the morning and then discovered my flight wasn't until the evening, which meant that I had nothing to do and nowhere to stay for the rest of the day while I was in Paris. 'Anything more I can do for you, Bill?' I asked, hoping, at least, that I'd be offered a room until my departure.

'No,' said Bill. 'Goodbye.'

So that was that; it had been nice but it was over. I later discovered that the reason I'd been asked to go along on the honeymoon was that Bill's then minder, who used to drive him everywhere, had written off the car – it turned over – and badly shaken Bill up, although mercifully no one sustained any injuries. Bill is a very cautious man in many ways: not only does he loathe flying, but he even hates driving fast and would make me stay at a maximum speed of 70 miles an hour, even when we were on the German autobahns and the rest of the traffic seemed to be driving twice as fast as us. Bill kept his minder on after the incident, but thereafter other people were brought in to act as chauffeur.

I didn't hear from Bill again until 1997, the year I met my wife Jane and the year I started my own business. Out of the blue came the call: would I drive Bill from Cheyne Walk, his London address, to his house in the South of France the next day? I would, so we started off at 7 a.m. and ended up at our destination at 11.30 p.m. that night, after one of the most shattering drives I have ever done in my life. We took it in turns to drive, with me aching to put my foot down on the accelerator and Bill making me creep along like an old lady, yelling in irritation if I ever went over 70. The journey was enlivened no end, however, by a conversation I had with Bill on the subject of Brian Jones, the original Rolling Stone who died of a drug overdose at the end of the 1960s.

'It was Brian who actually started the Stones, but Mick and Keith felt they should be in control of the band,' said Bill. 'Then Brian started on drugs, which meant that whenever TV and interviews came along, Brian was too out of his head to do anything, so it was always those two who appeared and got all the glory. Then it moved on to Anita Pallenberg. Brian really loved her but Keith fancied her, too. So Brian was increasingly pushed to the back of the band, lost his woman, got increasingly depressed, took more and more drugs and eventually had an overdose.'

'I see,' I said. We finally got to the house: I was put up in a local hotel (not, by a long shot, the nicest I've stayed in) and I then had to get up at the crack of dawn the following day to return to London, while Bill relaxed in the sunshine. There are many benefits to being a rich, internationally famous rock star.

There were several more mad dashes from London to France after that, as well as some work when Bill was in London, but it was only in 2001 when I went on tour with Bill and his band, The Rhythm Kings, that I saw he wasn't matey all the time. At first it was all right, with banter in the back of the car between Bill, his manager Tony Pancino and another member of the band. They'd spend their time eyeing up the women we passed and measuring up their attractiveness. 'Now that girl's pretty,' Tony would say. 'But young. Very young. Much too young for you, Bill. Whoops! What did I say!'

Bill took it in good heart. 'Definitely too young,' he'd say. 'I've learned my lesson there.'

It was also increasingly apparent who was a strong force in Bill and Suzanne's marriage. Suzanne had redecorated the house in exactly the way she wanted, and she was in control of the rest of their life, too. Tony and this other member of the band had arranged for two English girls who had never been abroad before to come out and spend a few days in the South of France. 'Can we use your Jeep, Bill?' Tony asked.

Bill looked shifty. 'I'll have to speak to Suzanne,' he

muttered and whipped out his mobile phone. A short conversation followed in which Suzanne made it clear what she thought about men flying English girls out to meet them and said that anyway Karen, a member of Bill's office was flying out and would need to use the Jeep. 'Sorry mate, no,' said Bill glumly when he came off the phone. *Oh dear*, I thought, *that was a loss of face in front of your friends ...*

In light of that, perhaps it wasn't very wise when, a couple of days later, Tony to ask if the four of them could come round to dinner so that the two young English girls could meet the famous ex-Stone. 'I'll have to speak to Suzanne,' said Bill, a mite wearily. The conversation was brief and, from what I could hear of it, tense. 'Sorry mate, no,' said Bill, even more glumly than before.

'You'll have to sort your missus out,' said Tony, who was clearly rather hurt, but determined to make a joke of it.

Obviously embarrassed, Bill called Suzanne and attempted to get her to change her mind, but to no avail. Suzanne was not having musicians and their young girlfriends in her house: she is as aware as anyone of her husband's controversial past and was clearly having no obvious reminders brought up in front of her. Bill tried to get his own back when she rang him later. Jerry Hall was staying in her house in St Tropez and was coming round to dinner at the Wyman's place. Would Bill make it back in time to be with them? 'No, you'll have to keep mine warm,' said Bill in a slightly doomed attempt to reassert his authority.

It during that time that I learned how much Bill hates flying. He was about to go on tour with his band in America, which meant that he was going to have to fly for the first time in nine years. 'I'm going to need a couple of Valium and a couple of vodkas before I can get on that plane,' he said. 'But it's better than when I was in the Stones. Then Mick would call me up and say I'd have to fly to America the day after tomorrow, which gave me no time to adjust to it. Now I'm my own boss, I don't fly if I don't want to.' That was the truth: the rest of the band had wanted to tour Japan, but Bill said no because of the flying that would ensue.

Bill could be unexpectedly kind and generous. Throughout the tour – and this irked me – no hotel rooms had been booked for me which, given the fact that I was Bill's driver, was very unprofessional of someone. Every time we reached a destination something would have to be sorted out and that usually caused difficulties: Bill's hotel would often be booked up and I'd have to find somewhere else to stay, which was time-consuming and inconvenient for all of us. On one occasion, though, when we got to a town in Austria late at night, Bill was desperate for a cup of tea, but his room had no tea-making facilities and the night porter at the desk did not speak good English. I went behind the scenes to the kitchen, but there was no one there, so I ended up going to an all night caf ... which was also no good. Finally I gave up and returned to the hotel. 'Sorry, mate, I can't find anything,' I said.

'That's okay,' said Bill and told me he'd booked me a room in my absence.

When I actually got there, it turned out to be a suite. I assumed it had been booked by mistake and rang Bill – who only had a room – immediately. 'Look Bill, I'll change with you,' I said when I told him what had happened.

'No, it's all right, stay there,' said Bill. 'Just don't mention it to the rest of the band.'

'But I can't! You should have it.'

'I mean it,' said Bill. 'Stay there. Enjoy it.'

And so I spent a couple of days in one of the most luxurious suites I've ever seen while Bill, bless him, made do with just a room. Mind you, it was a big room.

But these moments became increasingly rare as the more difficult side of Bill's personality began to show. Some problems that occurred between us were trivial. I was allowed to smoke in the car because Bill smoked too, but whereas he was allowed to open a window for the smoke to disappear, I wasn't. This meant I would be surrounded by waves of smoke that would only be released when Bill wanted them to be. Nor was I allowed to turn on the air-conditioning – or open a window – even when we were driving in sweltering temperatures through Spain. It became almost unbearable. 'I don't like the cold,' said Bill by way of explanation, 'because when I was a child, we were so poor we couldn't even afford enough blankets for all of us. Ever since then, I've never been able to take even the slightest chill.' I have nothing but sympathy for anyone who comes from an impoverished background, but in this case I was so hot I was scarcely able to drive. Bill would occasionally open the sun roof, but that just had the effect of letting even hotter air in to the car and burning the top of my head, while the rest of me stayed as boiling as ever. All in all, it was a great relief when the drive was done.

And then there were less trivial incidents. I was working for Bill, remember, which meant that even if we got on together, we were not exactly on equal terms. This first manifested itself in a funny (as in peculiar) way. I can't pronounce foreign place names very well, so I tended to read them out as I saw them on road signs. Bill used to pick me up on it all the time – and he wasn't doing it gently, either. We'd be going to Besancon: 'That's the turn-off to Bess-an-gon,' I'd say.

'I think you mean Besan-cion,' Bill would comment.

I pronounced Arhus in Denmark 'Are-huss' and got contradicted for that – the 'r' is silent – Bejle Begg-le and was informed that it was 'Beej', Munster as in the family and was told it was Muenster and many, many more. I wouldn't have minded, but Bill appeared to be putting me down and that showed whenever we reached our destination. We were always late because Bill wouldn't leave until at least an hour after we were supposed to and then he'd forbid me to drive fast on the motorways, but this amusingly became my fault when he was explaining himself to the band. 'Keith doesn't even know the names of the cities, let alone how to get here,' he'd say.

His manner also became increasingly abrupt. Bill is very fond of the sound of his own voice and once started rarely lets anyone else get a word in, but on the few occasions I'd say anything, there'd be an abrupt, 'What?' He was short and dismissive and increasingly attempted to put me down. I have no idea why this happened – we got on famously to begin with. Stars can be like this more than anyone: the more famous a person is, the more they can dread being seen at such close quarters. Perhaps that was the case with Bill.

Whatever the reason, though, finally Bill became completely contrary. One night when he was playing in Samso, a little island in Denmark, I wasn't required to drive him and so was sitting in the foyer of the hotel wearing a T-shirt, stonewashed jeans, stonewashed shirt and pointy-toed black boots. Remember, Bill didn't like to have men in suits around him and I was planning to go out later in the evening. However, when he saw me, he stopped abruptly. 'Exactly who's going on stage, me or you?' he asked and he did not appear to be joking.

I tried to laugh it off but Bill was having none of it. 'Have you seen what he's wearing?' I heard him say as he went off. One of the band members caught my eye and gave an embarrassed shrug.

Bill was in much the same mood the next morning when, not to put too fine a point on it, I saved his bacon. We were due to catch the ferry back to the mainland, after which we were to drive to Austria for a concert that night. We were misinformed though, and were told that the ferry departed from where it had dropped us; when we got there, no one was around except a little girl. I got out and asked her where the ferry was.

'The other side of the island, sir.'

We had ten minutes to get across the island to make it for embarkation time. There was nothing for it: I drove through the tiny roads like a mad thing. The only trouble was that, as you'll be aware by now, Bill hates speed. 'Keith! Slow down!' he kept yelling.

'I can't. You've got to get to that ferry. It's the only way off the island.'

We got there, Bill gripping his seat, and discovered it was

too late to embark. You need many qualities to be a driver and they don't all involve being able to move off sharply. You need to keep a clear head and be able to cope in an emergency. This was one of those occasions. I leapt out of the car and ran towards the men ushering the cars on board. 'I've got Bill Wyman in the back of the car and he's got to get to a concert in Austria tonight,' I gabbled.

The men looked doubtful. 'Well, we're trying to get a few extra cars on board, so you can go and join the queue,' one said and pointed to the relevant spot. I drove over and realised that there were five cars (we were the fifth) and three places left on the ferry so, while no one was looking, I suddenly sped out of the queue and drove past the other cars and on to the boat. The customs men tried to stop me but by then it was too late: we were on and I assumed (rightly) that they were very unlikely to go to all the bother of evicting a famous passenger from the boat. I turned to Bill, expecting a word of thanks. First there was a silence and then – 'Why were you driving like that!' he burst out. 'I told you to slow down!'

'I got you to the boat,' I said.

Bill said nothing – he simply turned away.

My wife Jane, who's also a driver, once ran into difficulties with the Wymans too. Jerry Hall holds regular sessions with a rabbi, in which everyone studies the kabbala, a form of

Jewish mysticism very popular with many celebrities such as Madonna. Suzanne regularly attends these sessions and Jane used to take her from the Wymans' place in Cheyne Walk to the Jagger residence in Richmond. On one occasion, Suzanne, without warning, asked Jane to take her first to Campden Hill in west London. The 'p' in Campden is silent and so Jane started off in the direction of Camden Town in north London.

It's an easy mistake and one that is Jane realised she'd made almost straight away, so she pulled over to consult the A-Z. Suzanne saw what she was doing and became annoyed. 'What are you doing? You look it up in the book, I'm getting a black cab,' she said and got out of the car. When you're a driver, that sort of behaviour puts you in an extremely difficult position. What are you supposed to do? Jane had been booked for the afternoon, so she decided to follow Suzanne to her destination and Suzanne agreed to be driven down to Jerry's. A message came back the next day, though, to the effect that Suzanne only wanted to be driven by me in the future, a message that caused Jane some relief.

Bill eventually gave up asking for either of us and I think that's because of the amount of time I spent with Mick. I wasn't employed full time by Mick, but he used me so much that I felt my loyalties lay towards him. This meant that if both of them wanted me at the same time I would drive Mick and send someone else to look after Bill. After being second best in the Stones for so many years, I suspect Bill refuses to be second best anywhere else after that, especially where Mick is concerned. Celebrities are often so competitive that even a little issue about who drives whom can blow up in to a crisis.

I prefer to remember the good times I had working for Bill – and there were many of them. One of my favourite memories is of driving through France at about 9 p.m. with a clear sky evening up above us. Quite suddenly a light appeared in the sky. We could tell it wasn't a star as it was too low, but neither was it a plane, because it was absolutely stationary. 'It's a UFO,' breathed Bill. Carefully, he took a camera from his bag, opened the sun roof and stood up on his seat, his head and shoulders above the roof, filming the mysterious object.

I was about to mock when quite suddenly it appeared in my mirror – and we were driving down a completely straight road. 'I've lost it!' shouted Bill. Then, just as suddenly, it disappeared from my view – 'Found it again!' cried a clearly excited Bill. Later on we discovered that there had been sightings of something in this part of France before and no one had ever been able to work out what it was.

At the time, we both felt childish excitement at our mystery find. And so we drove on, through the highways and byways of rural France, Bill standing on the seat filming an unidentified flying object. In a way, that was a fitting epitaph for our relationship: Bill was always curious about our surroundings, always eager to explore what else might be out there and it is satisfying to know that he could find happiness out of something as simple as a clear French night sky.

9

# In The Court of Queen Barbra

THESE DAYS, in a world where republics rather than monarchies are the norm, where the ancient aristocracy has no money and even less influence, celebrities have taken over where royalty left off. It is celebrities who live in vast houses with a huge personal entourage and it is celebrities who hold court for their admirers. And like any court, that of the celebrity contains friends and enemies, statesmen and sycophants, mighty rulers and humble carriagemen. And for the short time that I served in the court of Queen Barbra, the last of the above is exactly what I was.

The first time I met Barbra Streisand was in July 1992. Initially another driver had been assigned to her, but he forgot the cardinal rule when you are with a queen – never speak until you are spoken to – and she requested a replacement, which turned out to be me. (This same driver has been warned on a number of occasions about being a nuisance because he was talking too much and irritating his passenger: the rich are not just different from you and I because they have a lot of money, but also because they can be extremely anti-social. Only select members of the entourage are allowed to talk, and the person behind the wheel is rarely one of them.) This was some years before the queen chose her king and she was then dallying with a handsome prince – Andre Aggassi, the reason for her visit. He was playing at Wimbledon and she was there to see him. A commentator at the time said she, 'Looked at him like he was an ice cream cone with a cherry on top.' As for Barbra, she compared Agassi to a 'Zen master'. There has always been intensive speculation about the full nature of their relationship, Barbra being the best part of two decades older than Agassi, but I subscribe to the ice-cream theory.

I had heard that Barbra could be a tyrant to her staff but with me she was always both pleasant and polite. All I had to do on the first day was to drive her from The Berkeley, where she was staying, to The Dorchester, where he was said to be staying, wait for some hours and then take her back again. Even at that early stage, though, I noticed that what Barbra wants, Barbra gets. Everyone, but everyone, defers to her. And I got the Queen's approval: 'That was a lot better than yesterday,' she remarked when she got out of the car.

Barbra is a famous collector and the next day was spent shopping for antiques. She was looking for bric a brac and wanted to tour the famous districts: Bond Street and its environs, the Burlington Arcade, Pimlico and Islington, where Tony Blair and his family used to live. Sometimes she would come out of the shops carrying parcels and sometimes she would have the goods shipped back to one of her homes in the United States. By this time, however, the word was out that the Queen was in town and so began the familiar routine – familiar to both of us, although for different reasons – of dodging the cameras. Initially there were just a couple of snappers but gossip spreads fast and soon Barbra was surrounded wherever she went. 'Look guys,' she said finally, in that famous Brooklyn twang of hers, 'if I give you one picture, will you go away? Is that a deal?' The photographers agreed and so Barbra posed for a picture outside an antiques shop in Lowndes Street. They left us alone for a short time after that, but soon broke their word and caught up with her again in Pimlico, one of London's foremost antique districts. This time I was forced to get in the way: I blocked the cameras and Barbra, who was becoming quite agitated, made her escape.

That was Barbra on a private visit, but the next time I met her, a year later, she was on the celebrity equivalent of a state visit. Barbra was to be singing at four concerts in Wembley, her first live concerts in Britain for getting on for twenty years, and there was wild excitement in the media and amongst her fans surrounding the trip. It was also on this visit that I found out how very competitive it can get in Queen Barbra's court.

Barbra Streisand was born in Brooklyn on April 24, 1942, to Diana and Emanuel Streisand; her father died when Barbra was just fifteen months old. Educated at the Erasmus High School in Brooklyn, Barbra had an unusually distinctive voice from a very early age and won a singing contest at a club in Manhattan when still in her teens. Encouraged by this early success, she began to sing regularly at nearby clubs, such as the Blue Angel and Bon Soir. She made her Broadway debut in *I Can Get It For You Wholesale* when she was just nineteen, at around the time she signed up with Columbia Records; both of these achievements proclaimed a star in the making. Barbra won the New York Drama Critics Award and received a Tony nomination for her role on Broadway, while her debut LP, *The Barbra Streisand Album*, won two Grammy Awards in

1963, one of them for Album of the Year. At the time, she was the youngest artist to have received that award.

That led to the part which made Barbra in to an international star: Fanny Brice in *Funny Girl*. Barbra played the role in Broadway, gaining a second Tony nomination, and London and eventually went on to recreate the part in a 1968 film of the same name, for which she won an Oscar for Best Actress. Her other enormously successful films of the time included *Hello Dolly!*, *On A Clear Day You Can See Forever* and *What's Up, Doc?* before she won her second Oscar for *The Way We Were*. She went on to make *Yentl* in 1983, from a story by Isaac Bashevis Singer about a Jewish girl who disguises herself as a boy, and in so doing became the first woman to produce, direct, write and star in a major film. She then went one further with *The Prince Of Tides*, which was the first major film directed by its female star to receive a Best Director nomination – on top of seven more Academy Award nominations.

That roll-call of honours does not cover all the awards she has won or been nominated for throughout her career and on top of that there was her stunning successful singing career. Barbra describes herself as the 'actress who sings' but to me she's more the singer who acts. I love her music, as does the rest of the world. She is the highest selling female recording artist of all time and with forty-five gold albums is the second in the all-time charts, with only Elvis selling more. She has won innumerable awards for her singing career, culminating in Grammy's Lifetime Achievement and Legend Awards. Along the way she married and divorced Elliot Gould, by whom she has a son named Jason, became a gay icon, has donated huge amounts to charity and has become famous in every country in the world. All told, it's hardly surprising that the people who surround her behave as if they're in thrall to a medieval monarch – and that they become difficult and defensive when a newcomer is in their midst.

And it was ironic that it was Barbra's acolytes who were difficult to me rather than Barbra herself. In the show-business world, tales abound of Barbra's behaviour: she is said to be egotistical and self-obsessed, prone to losing her temper at the drop of a hat, a perfectionist, control freak and extremely temperamental. I did see some signs of this behaviour and I think it very unlikely that she would have got to the position she's now in if she hadn't had some of those characteristics, but such aspects of the Streisand personality were never, ever directed at me. It's very easy to take out your temper on someone who can't answer back and as a driver I've had to bite my tongue on numerous occasions with certain clients I could mention. But Barbra Streisand, although aware of her standing in the world, was nothing but decent to me. It was the people who worked for her who made my life a misery.

For a start, at Barbra's request I attended a meeting at The Dorchester as her driver a week before she arrived in order to sort out security details. When I walked in to the room, you could have cut the air with an axe. It was immediately clear that I was not wanted. 'I'm sorry, and you are?' said someone.

'Keith. Keith Badgery. I'm Barbra's driver.'

There was a muttering from somewhere. I later discovered that Barbra's own security people had wanted to pick her driver and so were annoyed that she had overruled them and requested me. 'Does the driver need to be here?' someone else asked.

'It's a meeting to talk about Barbra arrangements, so I've got to be here,' I said. 'Besides, she specifically requested my attendance.' I only just stopped myself from adding, 'So there.'

They couldn't really ask me to leave after that, but it set the tone for the whole stay. A week later I drove out to Heathrow to collect Barbra and, unlike the previous visit, there was a whole entourage of vehicles in tow, and not only those belonging to her. The crowds were unbelievable: fans were ecstatic that she was finally giving a live concert again and the press was going wild. I collected Barbra from the plane and attempted to escape the crowds but it was no use; we were followed by an army of cars and motorbikes all trying to get access to her and there was a near riot when the ever-vigilant paparazzi Richard Young and Dave Bennett skidded their shiny black BMW round in front of me at about eighty miles an hour in an attempt to get me to stop. But it was no good: I drove on while Barbra muttered to her assistant in the back. The poor woman was terrified, and not just because of the traffic. Barbra famously suffers from stage fright and at that point in the proceedings she was horribly nervous. You could practically feel the tension rolling in waves around the car; she had gone a slightly grey colour and was shaking visibly as Renate, her long-term assistant, tried to calm her down. Eventually we got to her hotel and Barbra disappeared inside. Nothing was seen or heard of her for the next couple of days.

All queens have a lady-in-waiting and Barbra is no different. Hers is the aforementioned Renate, who has danced in attendance on Barbra for many years now. It is also Renate who bears the brunt of Barbra's temper when anything is wrong and, feeling as stressed as she was, Barbra tended to take it out on her loyal aide during that trip to the UK. Barbra is very vain about her hands and indeed, she has beautiful long slim fingers which Renate would manicure in the back of the car as we roared through London. 'Not like that!' I could hear Barbra yelling. 'You've smudged it!' And there would be a long-suffering silence as Renate would start all over again. I ultimately came to the conclusion that she was responsible for Barbra's feeling of well being. It would be Renate who calmed her down when she was angry or upset, Renate who cheered her up when she was gloomy and Renate who made sure everything Barbra needed was immediately to hand.

I was with Barbra for fifteen days, in the course of which she did four performances. She was very quiet and because of her dreadful stage fright, scarcely left the hotel before the first of these performances, which was just as well from my point of view as I was having problems with the commander of her armed forces – or in modern parlance, her security chief Tony Quinn. For some reason Tony felt that I shouldn't have a laminate, the security pass that gives you full access backstage. It is absolutely standard practice for drivers to have laminates when they are driving a star, not least because the star might ask you to deliver something to his or her dressing room. It was a full two days before all my papers were finally sorted out, something that has never happened to me before or since in all my years as a driver.

Worse was to come but before that there was the first of Barbra's concerts. She wasn't the only one who wanted to get it over with; we all did. I drove her to Wembley for that first show. The only time she spoke was to snap at Renate and she was by now shaking quite violently. It must have been torture for her. At times she looked as if she was going to be sick. We finally got to Wembley; I didn't say anything, as I thought it better not to and the last I saw of Barbra before the show was as she slowly made her way to her dressing room escorted by the ever loyal and dependable Renate.

The show was an absolute triumph, as we all knew it would be. I was backstage throughout as Barbra's magnificent voice soared through Wembley, bringing the house down and the audience up on their feet; everyone loved her and she was given a standing ovation. Back in the car with her manager in tow, she was ecstatic. 'Was that good? Didn't that go well?' she asked and was reassured by her courtiers that she was wonderful. Then she leaned over the seat to me. 'What about you Keith, did you enjoy the show?' she asked.

'I thought you sounded amazing,' I replied.

'And how did it look from out front?'

I was a little embarrassed. I would have loved to have bought tickets for the show, but they were unbelievably expensive – something in the region of a couple of hundred pounds. 'Well you see,' I said awkwardly, 'I heard it all from backstage. I couldn't really afford ...'

'Oh,' said Barbra. 'Of course.' She turned back to chat to her manager and I thought no more about it until the next morning – when I received three tickets for the best seats in the house for the next concert.

That was a couple of days away, though, and before then I had my own problems to deal with at Queen Barbra's court. Along with Tony there were two more junior lieutenants. They were fine but Tony was not making life easy for me. For a start, he was insisting that if I were to drive Barbra, I had to be present at The Dorchester from 9 a.m. until 11 p.m. Like all good queens holding court, however, Barbra was receiving visitors rather than going out to greet them herself, and so I wasn't actually needed for any of this time. That wouldn't have mattered so much, though, if any arrangements had been made to look after me when I was there, but they hadn't – and because I was constantly on call, I couldn't even move from my post to get anything to eat.

Barbra knew nothing of any of this and I didn't like to say anything given that Tony was a long-term employee, so it was actually the manager of The Dorchester, Mr Obertelli who saved me. I'd met him in the past and when he saw I'd been hanging around for a couple of days he came over to ask what was happening. I explained the situation.

'I'm surprised they haven't laid on a room for you,' he said (this is standard practice for drivers and all the staff needed when a star is in town.)

'Barbra doesn't know they haven't and I can't tell her myself,' I said.

Mr Obertelli was extremely sympathetic. 'Look,' he said. 'I'll arrange for reception to give you a staff pass so you can use the staff canteen.' He did just that and so at least I was able to eat and hang around the hotel without feeling quite as conspicuous as I had in the lobby. The atmosphere of tension persisted, though – in some ways even more strongly than before.

More problems arose when the next concert came up, the one for which I had tickets. I was almost as excited as Barbra herself as I drove her to Wembley: I was taking my then girlfriend Gill and her mother Esme along with me. All three of us had been fans for years and were massively looking forward to seeing the show. After dropping Barbra at the stage door entrance, I made my way around to the front, where the two of them were waiting for me. We made our way to our seats, the lights went down … and then, quite suddenly, a representative from Barbra's record company appeared and asked us to leave because Paul Burger, the head of Sony, had suddenly and unexpectedly arrived. What could I do? I was only the driver. With a very heavy heart the three of us made our way to the exit while I tried to think of some treat I could give the two of them to make up for the disappointment.

Barbra was full of excitement when I met her after the show, beaming at everyone and even toning down her barked instructions to Renate as we set off back to the centre of town. 'So what did you think?' she asked. 'Did you like the seats?'

This time I decided I would tell her what had happened. 'Actually Barbra,' I began, 'we were asked to leave.'

'What?' demanded Barbra. 'Why? What happened?'

'Paul Burger turned up and they wanted the seats for him.'

There was a short and ominous silence from the back of the car followed by an explosion. 'What! This is outrageous! I'm going to do something about this!' yelled Barbra. 'I'm so sorry Keith, I had absolutely no idea. Renate! Listen!' And with that she barked a few orders, with the result that three tickets for three equally good seats were presented to me the following day. When that concert came about, no one asked me to move.

She was always very good to me, but as Barbra's confidence returned, so did her imperiousness. There was an air of sovereignty about her. She didn't lay down stern ground rules, but somehow people had a habit of falling at her feet – metaphorically, if not literally. Barbra was enormously rich and enormously famous, the two components that make a monarch in the entertainment world – and it showed. In fact, in many ways I suspect she receives more deference than many modern royals, as her patronage can mean an enormous amount to a career or a charity. Or perhaps people just like basking in the glow of reflected glory.

Barbra became increasingly happy and increasingly confident as her time here wore on, but for me the situation was to get no easier. We would use hand-held radios to communicate, in the course of which I got told off for using the word 'roger' as in 'roger and out.' 'Why do you have to keep saying that?' he snapped. (I had a feeling he'd heard that the word had other connotations in England and was worried that I was making a joke at his expense.)

'It's what people say when they use walkie-talkies Tony,' I replied.

The situation became slightly easier when the two lieutenants were replaced by two other men. Once, when Barbra was shopping for china in South Audley Street, Tony really did begin to make himself look over the top: he shoved on a pair of sunglasses and started walking up and down the street, even checking the rooftops, as if there would be hired assassins lurking behind every chimney pot. 'Who does he think he's guarding, President Clinton?' one of my new friends remarked incredulously. I couldn't have agreed with him more.

While Barbra was in situ at The Dorchester, she was forced to come and go via a car collecting her in the basement, which she didn't like at all, mentioning constantly how scruffy it was. However, there really was no alternative. Celebrities who reveal all to the press and then complain if something that they don't like is written about them are, quite rightly, held in contempt. But what people don't often realise is that life can be very problematic when you are as big a star as Barbra Streisand. She, like some of the other people in this book, simply can't do what she wants at the drop of a hat. Everything has to be prearranged and organised down to the last detail and Barbra must be protected from her adoring fans. While in London she wanted to see the Trooping of the Colour, but it was impossible because of security reasons. I did, however, drive her past the sights: Buckingham Palace, the Houses of Parliament and Westminster Cathedral. 'Isn't that beautiful,' said Barbra, now visibly relaxed and enjoying herself.

On her last night Barbra held a dinner at The Ivy, the restaurant that is a home-from-home for so many celebrities, where she entertained the likes of Donna Karan, the New York-based fashion designer, and Shelley Lazare, Barbra's manager. As I drove her back to the hotel that night, Barbra looked so contented that she was almost beautiful and I felt deeply honoured to have driven one of the greatest female singers of the twentieth century in this visit to a foreign land. And for the record, Barbra is a very attractive woman in person. Apparently she once contemplated having a nose job, but decided against it when she was told it might affect her singing voice. To be honest, I don't think she needs one. Her looks are distinctive and when she's in the right mood, very lovely. As her mother once said, why can't the world accept she has the voice of an angel? Is that really so much to bear?

10

# The Hands That Nearly Rocked My Cradle

SEX AND CELEBRITY, celebrity and sex. The two go hand in hand. If you are famous, people want to sleep with you. It's as simple as that. I have seen the celebrities I've driven propositioned on numerous occasions; sometimes the celebs have taken up the suggestion, sometimes not. And it's incredible the lengths people will go to in order to get close to a celebrity. Wives and girlfriends are ignored by women out on the prowl, as are husbands and boyfriends by predatory men.

Given the amount of temptation that crosses their paths, it's a wonder any celebrity relationship manages to last at all. Sandra Bullock attended the 2002 Oscars with Hugh Grant and recalled the amount of attention paid to her handsome friend. 'It was hysterical,' she says. 'We were standing at the bar and Uma Therman and Ethan Hawke came over. Uma looked so beautiful it was frightening, but it was Hugh and Ethan who got all the attention. Women flocked to them. It was phenomenal.'

I have seen all of this at close hand, from screaming crowds to girls hiding in the bushes waiting for Mick Jagger to come home. And celebrity rubs off on the people surrounding the glittering stars, too, with the result that they – or rather, we – get propositioned too. I've lost count of the number of times girls have forced their numbers on me just because I'm near someone famous and after a while I came to accept it as part of the job – not a bad part of the job, at that. There was one thing I wasn't prepared for though, and that was being propositioned by a celebrity herself. There is a fine line you don't cross over in this business; you don't get too close, you don't get too familiar and you assume the celebrities will behave in exactly the same way towards you. Sometimes, you are wrong.

It was July 1993 and I had an assignment I was looking forward to: I was to collect Rebecca De Mornay and drive her to Cornwall, where she would be filming *The Three Musketeers*. Rebecca had hit the big time a year earlier when she starred in *The Hand That Rocks the Cradle*, about a psychotic nanny who tries to destroy the woman who accused her (the nanny's) gynaecologist husband of abusing her. Rebecca was already known for her beauty, and I was looking forward to meeting her in the flesh. She didn't disappoint: she's a lovely looking woman, slim, with fair hair, and utterly natural and relaxed with it. 'Hi Keith!' she said as soon as we met, 'I'm Rebecca.' *This is going to be a very nice job*, I thought to myself.

We set off on the long drive south-west. Rebecca was tired after her flight but chatty and peckish: 'Could we stop at a service station, Keith?' she asked. 'I want something to eat.' We could and did and dressed as she was in old jeans and a T-shirt, no one recognised her, so she was able to buy a sandwich to eat in the car in peace. As we walked through the crowded station, she linked her arm through mine. *What a lovely, friendly lady*, I thought. I was also struck by the surreal aspect of the situation – walking through a crowded motorway station with a major Hollywood star on my arm – but I wasn't complaining.

Rebecca was chatty throughout the rest of the journey. She had been to England recently and was glad to be back, she said, and she also mentioned that she was looking forward to making the film. She told me about her upbringing, when she had also spent some time in England, and about the fact that she had once worked as a waitress in

London, something I found difficult to imagine. 'I love this country!' she said. 'It's so great!' Once we arrived at the hotel and she was greeted by a series of flunkies from the film company: 'We must have a pot of English tea!' said Rebecca. 'I'm just going to get my stuff up to my suite and then I'll be back down. See you in a minute!'

And so tea was served, with scones and cream and strawberry jam and all of us – Rebecca, myself and the film company flunkies – sat around as if we were at a civilised tea party in the eighteenth century rather than in the presence of a big star over from the States to make a big film. Rebecca was lapping it up. She wasn't so happy, though, when she discovered that she was staying at a different hotel from the rest of the cast, one that was seven or eight miles away from the centre of the action. 'And why exactly is that?' she demanded (even the nicest film stars can start acting like a diva at the drop of a hat.)

'We wanted to get a suite for you and there were no more suites in the other hotel.'

'Hmm,' said Rebecca irritably. 'Well, in that case I want a driver of my own throughout my stay here. You can't possibly expect me to be so far away from the others all the time.'

At this point I thought I'd better make a move. We were in the heart of Cornwall and I had a long drive back to London

– four hours if I was lucky – so I said I'd be on my way. Rebecca looked at me in disbelief. 'You mean you're going all the way back today?' she asked.

'Well yes,' I said. 'Unless you want something more from me, that is.'

'Why, you can't drive all that way tonight,' said Rebecca brightly.

'I've got to. My company will be expecting me back.'

'Won't you be too tired?'

'No, I'll be fine,' I replied. 'And anyway, I haven't got anywhere to stay down here. I'll have to get home so that I'll have a bed for the night!'

I had meant that last bit as a joke, but Rebecca looked thoughtful. 'Tell you what,' she said after a moment, 'I've got a second bedroom in my suite. You can stay here.'

I felt a bit flabbergasted and didn't know what to say. In my years in the business, I'd had fans flinging themselves at me but never the star herself. That is, if that's what she was doing; when you're in a situation like that, you're not sure if you're misreading the signs – and if you were to do so, it really could result in a disaster. *Turn it in to a joke, old son*, I said to myself. *Make a laugh out of it, then you won't upset anyone.* 'Why Rebecca,' I said as lightly as I could, 'you wouldn't like the publicity that would go along with that.'

'Oh, I can handle that,' said Rebecca, equally lightly. 'The bed's there if you want it.'

'Really,' I said, 'I'd better go. My company will be expecting me and there will be trouble if I don't get back.'

'Absolutely,' said Rebecca heartily. 'You have a good drive back.'

We looked at each other. 'Well, bye!' I said at last. And, feeling utterly dumbfounded, I left.

Over the months that followed, I often thought to myself: *Was that my imagination? Rebecca De Mornay? I must have been dreaming*. However, she made two further visits over the course of the next two years which made me think.

The second visit happened a year after the first and although I only saw her fleetingly, she did, at least, make me feel wanted. I'd gone to the airport to pick her up and drive her to The Savoy. When she saw me, you'd have thought she was greeting her long-lost brother. 'Keith!' she squealed and threw her arms around me. 'How great to see you! How've you been doing?' And so it went on, all the way in to London: 'I'm so pleased you came to meet me,' she kept saying. She didn't, alas, invite me in to The Savoy – this time I'd have been a bit quicker off the mark – but she did make me feel that she was at least pleased to see me. And she was as friendly and chatty and beautiful as ever. I was delighted that we had, at least, bumped in to one another again.

This, incidentally, was not enough to convince me that I'd been right about our first meeting. It was her behaviour the next time we met, so in contrast to that on the previous two occasions, that got me wondering whether I had been reading the signs or indulging in wistful thinking.

It was a couple of months later. Leonard Cohen was flying in to the country and I was sent to meet him. I had no idea that he and Rebecca were an item so I was totally unprepared to see her walking down the steps of the plane behind him. Neither of us said anything other than hello when the two of them got in to the car and, given that both were asleep within a couple of minutes, there was no need for me to worry about whether I was supposed to involve them in conversation or not. Rebecca had given absolutely no indication that she knew who I was and, indeed, I was almost beginning to wonder if she'd forgotten me. We had met on a couple of occasions by this time, though, and had shared that long drive to Cornwall, so I was pretty sure that she must have had some inkling as to who I was.

I took them to The Westbury Hotel and the next day I took Leonard out to a series of appointments. Rebecca wasn't with him and I later learned that she'd phoned my office to see if I could take her out on a shopping trip. When she was told that I was in fact already out, she left a message for me: 'Could you just say thank you to Keith and I will speak to him over the next few days.' 'What did she mean by that, Keith?' asked a puzzled colleague.

'I've no idea,' I replied.

As it happens, when I took Leonard back to the hotel, Rebecca came down to talk to me before I'd driven away. 'I'm really grateful to you for not saying anything at the airport, Keith,' she began.

'Well, I wouldn't have said anything. It's not etiquette,' I replied.

'Yes, but thank you anyway.'

For the rest of their stay I drove Leonard around, occasionally bumping in to Rebecca and feeling rather miffed that I may have let such a prize escape my grasp. But these things happen, as Rebecca herself acknowledged in a note she sent to me at the end of her visit, thanking me for being so professional and telling me I'd made her stay that bit more comfortable. It was a nice thing to do and characteristic of a generous lady.

So I got some consolation in knowing I did the right thing. And yet still I think – if only!

\* \* \* \* \*

Another of my clients who might have had an interest in something other than my driving was a very different prospect indeed – Christopher Ciccone, Madonna's brother. I met them both in 1992, when Madonna came to this country on tour.

My first glimpse of both of them was at the airport. Madonna wafted past and although she was a nice-looking woman, for some reason I never took to her. There was something very cold and very aloof about her: she didn't bother with small talk – in fact, I don't think she even knew our names. In a job like mine, you don't exactly expect to become best friends with the people you're dealing with, but you do at least hope for the basic courtesies – which, in Madonna's case, we didn't really get.

Then again, 1992 was her most notorious year, the year in which the book *Sex* came out, filled with graphic images of Madonna naked in the unlikeliest of places – strolling down a busy road, for example – and so perhaps her public bad behaviour was spilling over in to her private life at the time. We didn't see a great deal of her – she was having a flirtation with one of her dancers and her troupe spent most of the time in the hotel, partying it up.

At first I was driving Freddie De Mann, Madonna's manager, but after a couple of days I was promoted to looking after Christopher. He was very different from his sister: very quiet and very shy. I liked him much more than his famous sibling. He looked after her, constantly fussing over her clothes and make-up and what was going on in the shows. This was when Madonna was going through her wildest period in her act as well: she was spitting and swearing at the audience when she was on stage and her act was becoming so obscene the Department of the Environment was called in. They warned her to stop the provocative behaviour and bad language on stage and threatened to close down the show if she didn't comply. Christopher reminded her of this just before she went on stage. 'I'll fucking do what I want,' said Madonna, who was clearly delighted at all the publicity. She did exactly as she had done the previous night – and no one closed down the show. Middle England might have been outraged, but Madonna was doing what Madonna did best and garnering huge amounts of money in to the bargain.

Christopher was an extremely good-looking man: women loved him and made a big fuss over him, but I'm afraid it was a waste of time on their part. One hot day during the summer, I drove him down to Liphook in Surrey, where he was visiting some friends. When we got to our destination, I found a lovely farm house complete with swimming pool – and two good-looking men in their twenties were frolicking in the pool. In the background, a couple of other people were having lunch. Christopher quickly changed in to his swimming trunks and dived in, as I loitered in the

187

background, unsure of what I should be doing. 'Come on in Keith, the water's great!' he yelled.

I laughed. 'Sorry, mate, I don't have any trunks on me,' I replied.

'We can lend you a pair of trunks,' said one of the boys in the pool.

'Thanks very much but –'

'Come on Keith, why not?' asked Christopher. By this time the three of them were throwing a big beach ball across the pool: there was a lot of shouting and laughter as they splashed about in the water.

'No really, I –'

'Come on Keith! Come on Keith!' they all shouted. I didn't in the end – not because they clearly weren't the marrying kind, but because I felt it wasn't my place. Instead, I went off and had lunch with some cows in the next field, which turned out to be equally pleasant. I'm a bit of a nature lover, when all's said and done.

When we got back to London that night, one of the more persistent paparazzi found out what it was like to get on the wrong side of Madonna. He'd been chasing her round London all day and after Madge, Christopher and their entourage had dinner that night, they went on to a nightclub. The irritating pap followed, cutting other cars up and making a danger of himself in traffic as we all went on our way. Finally, he nearly knocked over a biker in Hyde Park. The biker followed and the second the pap's car stopped, he nearly smashed the window in, something we felt the sleazy snapper deserved. He continued to follow us, though, and when we got to the nightclub, Madonna had had enough. She had a word with the doorman, who came out and grabbed the paparazzo's keys out of the ignition. 'You are not going anywhere,' he said. Then just to make the point, we all let his tyres down. He stayed away from us for a few days after that.

As for Madonna herself, I never did take to her, although from what I can tell she seems a nicer woman these days. Marriage and children must have calmed her down. She wasn't calm back then, though, as I discovered on the only day I drove her. Her regular driver was an old friend of mine, affectionately known as Stan the Man, and one day, when she was visiting a dance studio in north London, we agreed he'd take her usual car and distract the paparazzi, while I collected her from the back of the hotel and took her on to her destination. We had several more cars waiting for us along the route, so that whenever we had to stop at traffic lights, they could pull up behind us and stop the paparazzi from getting in too close.

Madonna was in the back of the car with her PR woman, paying absolutely no attention to me, until we got in to the further reaches of north London. 'What goes on in this place?' she demanded, wrinkling her nose.

I racked my brains. 'Arsenal football ground is nearby,' I said.

It was the only thing I could think of, but Madonna looked completely bemused. I tried again. 'And Holloway women's prison is nearby too,' I added.

Madonna sat up. 'Really?' she asked.

'Yes, that's it over there.' I pointed to a red building jutting in to the street.

Madonna exchanged glances with her PR woman. 'Shall we go and get a takeaway?' she asked.

# Pretty
# Women

I'VE BEEN LUCKY enough to meet a number of divas in my time as a driver, women who often came from dirt poor backgrounds and, through sheer ambition, determination and talent, made it to the very top of the tree.

I met the most famous of these divas in February 1994 although I didn't know until the very last minute I was going to do so. I met a Miss Elaine Goldsmith and various people from Warner Brothers at Heathrow one day and after they had unwound at The Dorchester, I spent the day showing them around Cambridge. I soon started getting on very well with Elaine and at one point she commented, rather mysteriously, 'My client will like you. I can tell that by the way you are.'

It was news to me that she had a client – I had thought I was just looking after her group. Now, of course, I realise I was being tested and clearly I passed because late that night I was told to go and pick up a security guard called Elvis the following morning at 4 a.m. and then proceed to Luton airport to collect ... Julia Roberts. Elaine was Julia's agent. No matter how long you've been in the business, you can't help but be excited when you're going to meet a really big star and I was absolutely thrilled at the prospect.

Julia was actually born Julie Fiona Roberts in 1967 in Atlanta, Georgia. Her parents are Walter Roberts, a vacuum cleaner salesman, an actor and a writer and Betty, a church secretary and an actress. The couple founded the Atlanta Actors and Writers Workshop in the 1960s. Julia's sister Lisa and her brother Eric are actors too. 'They were dirt poor when Julia was growing up,' says Thomas Caldwell, a friend of the Roberts family. 'In fact, her parents were so poor that Martin Luther King Jr and his wife, Coretta, paid the hospital bills for Julia's delivery. Coretta was a casual friend of Julia's mother. She made the offer, and Betty graciously accepted it. In years to come, there was no money for food. Julia said that she ate a lot of peanut butter sandwiches, with ham and cheese on special occasions. She went hungry so many times that she vowed that she would never be broke again.'

Walter and Betty divorced in 1971 when Julia was four, after Betty had an affair with Michael Motes, who became her second husband. The whole family split up. Walter and Eric stayed in Atlanta, while Julia moved with her sister Lisa and her mother to Smyrna. The situation was to create a yearning for a father figure in Julia that has never really been satisfied – and was perhaps the reason that I got on so well with her, as I tried to look after her. 'I think Julia always blamed our [natural] father, feeling that he should have made more of an effort to keep her,' says her brother Eric. 'Julia loved him so much. I think she felt abandoned.' I believe the situation got even worse. Betty wanted Julia to accept Michael as her father and so tried to bar contact with Walter – whom Julia adored – once even hiding a gold bracelet he sent her for Christmas, and telling her he'd forgotten to send a present.

Julia's childhood was very unhappy. Walter died five years later when Julia was only ten and there was even a debate about whether she should be allowed to attend the funeral. She did, but her mother had not allowed the young girl to see her father again before he died, possibly because he filed charges alleging that Julia was being treated badly. 'Julia is an innocent child who needs tenderness, and she's not getting it,' her father complained. 'I do not want her to suffer as an adult for anything that happens to her as a child.' Certainly Julia loathed her stepfather; while not physically abusive, he did not make her feel loved. This also influenced her views on men. 'Once, Julia's former fiance and actor Kiefer Sutherland seemed as if he was about to strike Julia during a fight,' says Thomas Caldwell. 'She screamed at him: "Don't even think about it. I will never allow a man hit me. I'll cut you off at the knees."'

After graduating from Campbell High School in 1985, Julia moved to New York where she joined her older sister Lisa in order to pursue an acting career. At first, she worked as a model. Her first big screen part came in 1986 with the western *Blood Red*. Her brother Eric had already made several films and been nominated for an Oscar for his role in Andrei Konchalovsky's *Runaway Train* with Rebecca De Mornay and Jon Voight. In *Blood Red*, Julia only played a small part as the sister of her brother Eric who was the leading man.

Julia's acting debut before an audience came in 1987 with the TV series *Crime Story* in which she played a teenager who has been sexually abused. The producer Michael Mann later also gave her a part in an episode of his *Miami Vice* TV series, in which she played a gangster's secretary who gets involved with Sonny Crockett (Don Johnson). During the next year and a half, the former 'Miss Panthera' from

Smyrna auditioned for TV commercials and film parts. After an appearance in the TV series *Spenser: For Hire*, she was finally offered larger roles.

Julia's first bigger part was in 1987 with *Satisfaction*, a film considered to be the vehicle to stardom for the leading woman of the sitcom *Family Ties*, Justine Bateman, though the teenage comedy was nothing to be proud of. On the set, the twenty-year-old Julia fell in love with fellow actor Liam Neeson – twice her age – with whom she lived for some time in Venice. It proved to be the first of many romances with her leading men. Since that time, of course, Julia has become the biggest female star in the world – although her love life remains as turbulent now as it was then.

Julia wasn't quite as big a star when I met her as she is now, but I'd loved her in *Pretty Woman* and I was really looking forward to meeting her. In person, Julia didn't disappoint. At about 5'5", she's a little smaller than you'd expect, as so many celebrities are, but she's stunning. Even when she's looking tired, as she was when she came off the plane, she still has that amazing smile, to say nothing of a slim figure, wonderful bone structure and that amazing hair. She's also extremely friendly – as soon as we were introduced, she threw her arms round me and gave me a little cuddle. My heart was definitely beating a little faster than usual as I drove her back to the Halcyon Hotel.

Julia's visit to London was supposed to be a secret one, while she held a series of meetings about a future film in which she was to star called *Mary Reilly*. Given that much of her stay in England involved meetings at The Dorchester, though, it was inevitable that she would be spotted and in no time the chase was on. This involved swift action on our part, which was difficult as it was Elvis's first close-up security job and he wasn't yet used to the pitfalls of the trade. On our second morning, Julia emerged from her hotel with curlers in her hair, clearly not a time at which she'd want to be photographed. It was me who noticed the cameraman present; I had to jump out of the car and block his lens while Julia leapt in. By the time we got to The Dorchester it was crawling with press so we smuggled Julia in through a back door: that evening, we had to stage an elaborate ruse whereby a big official limo was at the front, Julia sneaked out in an ordinary car, I followed and before the press had gathered what was happening, she got in to my car and we were off. 'Whose idea was that?' she asked.

'Mine, actually,' I said.

'Well it worked,' she replied.

Julia was looking for a flat to rent when she returned to make *Mary Reilly* and we found one almost immediately on Holyrood Road, just off the Fulham Road. It was a big, airy place, painted white with brass fittings, big plants and electric gates to the garage. The security was good and so she took it. And then, almost as soon as suddenly as she arrived, it was time for Julia to go home again. 'Keith, when I come back, you are going to drive me,' she said as we drove to the airport. 'Unless you've found some young chick to be with and don't want me any more.'

'I'm saving myself for you, Julia,' I told her.

'I'll hold you to that,' she said, and when we got to Luton, I was delighted to receive another kiss and a cuddle from the beautiful star. It was the last time I saw her, I'm afraid. She actually ended up being driven by Mick Devine, the Irish chauffeur she turned to after splitting up with Kiefer Sutherland, whom she was due to marry in 1991. The two have since become firm friends.

\* \* \* \* \*

Mariah Carey is the biggest selling female recording artist of the 1990s. She has sold 120 million albums and singles and despite her recent troubles – a breakdown and a split from her new record label, EMI – remains one of the major stars on the show business scene. Mariah has had 14 number one records on the Billboard Hot 100 singles chart and spent a total of sixty weeks at the top of that chart, a record. She also wrote every single one of those hits herself, with the exception of her cover version of the Jackson 5's 'I'll Be There'. I met her when she was just starting out, though, when she seemed to be little more than a shy little girl. I had no idea how big she would become but I witnessed the transformation – from disco baby to diva.

I first met Mariah Carey in 1991. At the time she was a little-known singer in England and as I picked her up from the airport with her entourage of just four people – hairdresser, make-up artist and two dancers – I found myself wondering, *Who's she?* The five of them piled in to the back of my Daimler limo, looking like nothing so much as a group of excited youngsters on their first trip abroad. Mariah herself appeared to be rather shy. I took them to The Mayfair Hotel, which is a nice hotel in London but not absolutely the tops, and dropped them off, wondering what on earth they were all doing here. The next day I found out.

I drove the five up to the Pebble Mill studios in Birmingham. They were all chatting away in the back of the car, talking about America and their boyfriends – I, like the rest of the world, had no idea who Mariah was going out with – while Mariah issued instructions about what they were going to do when they got to the studio. When we arrived, I followed them in, curious to see what Mariah was going to do. I knew she was a singer, but I didn't know a great deal more than that. And then, quite suddenly, Mariah came on to sing. She opened her mouth and launched in to 'Emotions' – and the hairs on the back of my neck stood up. I couldn't believe that this shy little girl had a voice like that; I later discovered she has a seven-octave range, which is extremely unusual, even amongst very famous singing stars.

From then on, Mariah was much more relaxed and confident. 'How was it, how did it look, Keith?' she asked when she came off the set.

'Fabulous,' I replied. 'I didn't know you had a voice like that.'

'Why, thank you Keith,' she replied.

The mood became increasingly jolly as the trip went on. The five of them would sing and dance in the car as I drove them around London, unless Mariah was going to a performance, in which case she would warm up her voice by going through her singing exercises in the car. 'I do apologise for my screeching,' she would say. And she seemed quite awestruck at the hand life had dealt her. 'You know, Keith, I used to be a waitress in New York before someone heard me sing,' she once told me. 'I just can't believe that everyone's making this fuss about me, laying on a car like this and everything.'

In due course, I began to learn more about Mariah's background. She was born on March 27, 1970, in New

York City, to a half-Venezuelan father, and an Irish mother, which accounts for her extraordinary looks. Racial prejudice was still very prevalent at the time, though – Mariah's mother, Patricia, an opera singer and vocal coach, was disowned by her family when she married Alfred Carey, an aeronautical engineer. The neighbours were no better and the family had its cars blown up and dogs poisoned during Mariah's early years.

Sadly, the strain took its toll on the marriage and Patricia and Alfred divorced when Mariah was only three. Patricia had realised, though, that her daughter had a real gift and began to give her lessons at home. Mariah sang for friends, performed in talent shows and at folk-music festivals and by the time she entered junior high, she had begun to write and compose her own songs.

When she was a teenager, Mariah started studying music professionally and moved to Manhattan in 1987. Mariah began singing as a part-time backup singer with the rhythm-and-blues singer Brenda K Starr, while working as a waitress to make ends meet – she claimed that twenty restaurants had fired her because of her 'bad' attitude, although she was always perfectly all right with me.

It was while working with Brenda that Maria got her big break: she got close enough to Colombia boss Tommy Mottola to slip him a demo tape. Tommy acted fast. He signed Mariah up immediately and, just ten months after she moved to Manhattan, she released her first album in 1990. It sold over six million copies and went to number one.

I knew nothing of this as I took Mariah and her entourage on a trip around London, showing them sights such as Buckingham Palace, Westminster Cathedral, Big Ben and the Tower of London; to me, they were just a bunch of fresh-faced kids. Mariah was greatly excited when I stopped on London Bridge for her to take pictures – technically it's illegal – and rather shocked when I began telling her about England's history.

'What went on in the Tower?' she asked.

'It's where they beheaded people.'

Mariah was horrified. 'No! That doesn't happen in England, does it?'

'Not any more, but it used to. And you know what they did to some traitors?'

'What?'

'They would chain them to the banks of the Thames, so that when the water level rose with the tide, they'd drown.'

'Euow! No! I don't believe it! Oh that's so gross!'

Once she got over our barbaric history, though, Mariah fell in love with London. She particularly liked Trafalgar Square, especially Nelson's Column and the lions. 'Your architecture here is so great,' she would say. 'I can't believe that a little while ago I was a waitress and now I'm seeing stuff like this. We don't have anything like this in the States. Don't you think it's so great, you guys?' Her friends would agree and there'd be much commenting on the sights until they went back to singing, dancing and talking about their boyfriends.

On the last day of her visit, I drove Mariah to the airport. She was dressed entirely in leather and for the first time I began to realise what a spectacularly beautiful woman she is. Often celebrities whom I don't know that well would jump out of the car without saying anything, but Mariah didn't. She hopped out, headed towards the door of the VIP lounge and then turned back and gave me a little wave. At that moment, she looked exactly like what she was back then: a sweet, shy little girl.

Times change. The next time Mariah came to Britain a few months later, to appear on *The Des O'Connor Show*, the was a visible difference in her. She was much more relaxed with the treatment she was receiving and there was no more talk about her past as a waitress. A lot had been going on in the States in those months: her album *Emotions* had been a huge success and Mariah was making the transition from up-and-coming singer to superstar. She was still friendly: 'Hi Keith, how ya been?' she asked before giving me a peck on the cheek. There were no more jolly sing-songs in the back of the car, though, and no cheerful talk about America and boyfriends. Mariah was on her own now, and concentrating on business.

I was very busy with Mick and Rod back then, so I didn't see Mariah again until some years later. When I finally did, the situation couldn't have been more different. For a start she was staying at The Lanesborough, one of London's smartest – and most expensive – hotels. Secondly, her entourage had grown. Whereas before everyone had bundled in to the back of the limo, now everyone got their own car. Her entourage had grown from four to twelve, with five cars and two people carriers to ferry everyone around. And Mariah herself was no longer the sweet little girl she used to be. There are two words to explain this: Tommy Mottola. Her boss was now her husband and he wanted nothing but the best for his biggest star.

This was 1994. The year before, Mariah and Tommy formalised their relationship. Inspired by the wedding of Prince Charles and Lady Diana Spencer – perhaps unwisely, given the outcome of that marriage – the couple spent $500,000 on their wedding in June 1993. There were fifty flower girls, an eight-piece orchestra, and a boy's choir alongside a 300-strong guest list including Bruce Springsteen, Barbra Streisand, Robert De Niro, and Ozzy Osbourne. 'When I look back and think about it, it's so unbelievable! I mean, it really is like Cinderella,' said Mariah and the couple – she was twenty-four and he was forty-four when they wed – went to live in a large mansion outside Manhattan.

But the marriage went the way of Charles and Diana's and in March 1998, Mariah flew to the Dominican Republic to obtain a divorce. She then flew to Tampa, Florida, to watch baseball player Derek Jeter, with whom, she had been romantically linked, though that romance too fizzled out. 'Media pressure was too much for them as a couple,' said a spokesperson for Mariah.

It was a long way from the little girl I had known, who was so excited about driving around London and who couldn't believe that she so recently had been a waitress, but the signs were there on that last trip. Success has many benefits, but it can harm you as a person and is no good at all for your long-term relationships.

\* \* \* \* \*

I drove Celine Dion purely by chance, when she was over in this country in the early 1990s, for the release of *Beauty and The Beast*. Like Bill Wyman, Celine was an extremely cautious passenger and the poor woman had initially been allocated a driver who fell asleep at the wheel. It was when they were on their way to Scotland and it happened only momentarily, but he lost control of the car. Celine was terrified and demanded someone else, hence the fact that I was drafted in to drive her. She remained an extremely nervous passenger, constantly checking to make sure that I was driving no faster than seventy miles per hour – just like Bill Wyman, in fact.

Again, as with Mariah, I had never heard of Celine before she was here, but when I heard her singing, it sent a chill down my spine. 'You have an amazing voice,' I said to her as we drove down to Birmingham. 'Oh Keith, that's so nice of you to say so. Could you slow down a little? You're going really fast.'

Poor Celine could not get over that driver falling asleep and talked about it endlessly. The person she talked about it to most of all was her manager Rene Angelil, who was with her on the trip. They were not yet officially a couple but I guessed something was afoot because I saw them holding hands in the back of the car. Our next journey was to Eastbourne to attend the Sony music convention. We were supposed to set off at 5 p.m., but in true diva style, we actually didn't get going until 10.30 that night. Celine and Rene were in the back of the car; after a while, they had both nodded off to sleep. This was an incredible compliment to me, as Celine never sleeps in cars. Both of them woke up just as we were getting to Eastbourne: 'Say Keith, I had a little nap,' she said.

'Did you enjoy it?' I asked.

'Oh yes.'

'Good. I had a little nap, too ...'

'Oh Keith!' Celine exclaimed.

\* \* \* \* \*

I have driven Shirley Bassey a number of times over the years and I had an experience with her that still makes a glow of embarrassment appear on my cheeks. Once, when we were driving past Sunburry on the M25, we were in the region of a sewage works. 'Oh my God!' screamed Shirley from the back. 'What is that smell?'

'It's a sewage works, Shirley,' I said. 'I'll drive as fast as I can.'

I put my foot down, sped away and would have thought no more about it were it not for the fact that the next time I drove Shirley, I had a badly upset stomach. I did everything I could to keep the situation under control but finally I could stand it no longer and quietly passed wind. A moment later, Shirley, who had been dozing, opened her eyes. 'Keith, are we going past one of those sewage works again?' she demanded.

I looked at the open fields on either side of the car. 'Yes

Shirley,' I said firmly. 'It's a long way away but yes, we are.'

Shirley looked at my face in the mirror and then the unbroken countryside sweeping for miles around. 'Yes, Keith,' she said.

\* \* \* \* \*

Perhaps my very favourite pretty woman was the Cuban-born singer Gloria Estefan. So many people in the world of show business are nice to you as and when it suits them and merely use other people to get their own way, but Gloria and her husband Emelio were a delight. I drove them in June 1993 when their regular driver was in Europe with Take That and the first thing I noticed was how warm and loving they are to one another – clearly a very happy couple.

On their first night in town, the couple wanted to visit the Hard Rock Cafe... with a member of their record company. I drove them to the restaurant, where they were dismayed to see a queue that looked about a mile long. 'Oh Lord, what are we going to do?' asked Gloria, looking dreadfully disappointed. 'We can't stand out here in the street.'

As it happens, I knew the doorman, Charles. 'Don't worry, I'll sort it,' I said and went and had a quick word. The party was ushered in without more ado. 'Park the car and we insist you join us,' said Gloria and so I spent the night at an adjacent table, as there was nothing available to fit all of us.

This pattern was repeated during the length of their stay here. Gloria was spending some days in Sir George Martin's studio in north London recording her latest album of Latin American music; the long and tedious hours I had to spend in the car outside came to an abrupt end when Emilio invited me to join them in production in the studio. In the evenings I would take them to a Lebanese restaurant in London's Shepherd's Market and each night they would insist that I eat with them. During those evenings Gloria confided that they had still not given up trying for a baby (the couple have been married since 1978, which gives you some idea of how unusual their relationship is in the music industry) and further admitted that she still suffered back pains from the dreadful bus accident she'd had in 1990 when she broke her back. 'But you know, Keith, I don't like to let the public see that,' she once told me.

This is extraordinarily generous behaviour from someone in an industry which looks on the supporting players as largely unimportant, but it was typical of the Estefans. Before they left, Gloria told me, 'We own a hotel in Miami, Keith, so if you ever want a nice vacation in Florida you'd be very welcome there.' I never took them up on this invitation and, alas, I never saw them again.

# Hollywood Greats

IN THE COURSE of my career as a driver, I've got to know some of the greatest figures in show business. Some of these, like Mick and Rod, have turned in to long-term acquaintanceships, while others have been just like ships passing in the night. But they have provided me with some very happy memories and a brief glimpse in to the lives of some of our best-known stars. My job was enjoyable at the best of times, but I never imagined when I was growing up that I would one day meet some of the most famous people in the world. It's just another perk.

One of the most famous and well-loved men I ever met was the late actor Jack Lemmon, famous for his brilliant performances in *Some Like It Hot, The Odd Couple* and many, many more outstanding films. I had been a fan of his for years and had heard many reports that Jack, unlike some of the younger and more conceited generation of stars, was a kind, decent and modest man. There is a type of American who makes you think of home on the range and apple pie and Jack Lemmon was very definitely that type of American.

Jack was in London in May 1994 to promote the film *Grumpy Old Men*, in which he starred with his long-term friend and acting partner Walter Matthau. Jack flew in to London on Concorde with his wife Felicia Farr and the two of them appeared looking like any elderly American couple on holiday in London: they held hands as they made their way to the car and fussed over one another once placed inside. 'Oh my, isn't it great to be here?' Jack asked as I drove them to their hotel. 'But I can't believe they're making such a fuss of me.' He never could see why people would pay him such a lot of attention and why film companies would lay on limousines, first-class travel and luxury hotels for him: as far as Jack himself was concerned, he was just a normal American boy who had had an exceptionally lucky life.

The couple rested that day before going out on a shopping spree the next day. Jack was deeply shocked by London prices – not for him the Hollywood habit of flashing his credit cards around. 'Do you know how much that hotel room costs?' he asked me in bewilderment. 'Do you know how much it costs to have dinner in that hotel?'

'I would have thought your film company would pay for it,' I said.

'Why yes, they do, but I still can't believe they have to pay those prices. And the shops! Have you seen how much everything costs in the shops? I can't believe the prices in this town. I think I'm going to have to put off shopping until I get home.'

'Jack honey, now you're beginning to sound like a real grumpy old man,' said Felicia, giving him a quick squeeze in the back of the car.

'No!' cried Jack with mock indignation. 'That's Walter! He's the real grumpy old man. Really, he should be here promoting the movie, not me.'

Jack was very modest about his incredible career as an actor. He had none of the airs and graces you see in so many younger stars and he took nothing for granted. He was constantly amazed that anyone should feel he had anything to say that was of interest and would simply mutter self-deprecatingly when told what a great actor he was and was intensely touched by the fuss people made of him. James Stewart's wife once famously told him to stop being James Stewart when he edged too close to his public persona (the anecdote he was telling at the time was becoming too long winded and James was milking it for all it was worth) and Jack Lemmon is also exactly what you would expect him to be: quietly spoken, polite and devoted to his wife, none of which are qualities that you often find in world-famous stars.

Jack was also still friends with Tony Curtis, with whom he co-starred in *Some Like It Hot*, although the two could not have been more different. After an early and disastrous first marriage, Jack wed Felicia in 1962 and theirs was a famously happy union. Tony on the other hand went through a string of wives, the latest being Jill Vanden Berg who was twenty-nine to Tony's seventy-four when they married in 1998. Her flamboyant dress sense is more than matched by his: together the couple would parade around town together, Jill sporting dresses split to the navel (or so it sometimes appears, at any rate) and Tony showing off his legs in shorts and sandals, which is not always the best of ideas for a man of his age. It was inconceivable to think of Jack behaving like that. Nor is that the only difference in their appearance. When you meet Tony there's a certain floridness to his complexion while his cheeks and neck are fleshy, a testament to his well-known liking for illicit substances – even if that particular aspect to his wild living is now in the past. Jack, on the other hand, looked as if he's spent most of his life feasting on milk and cookies. Nevertheless, the two were still friends, as I found out on that visit.

'I've heard Tony is in town, is that right?' Jack asked me as we drove around London together.

'I don't know, but I'll make enquiries.'

I did and Tony wasn't. 'Oh that's a big shame,' said Jack, looking crestfallen. 'I was hoping to catch up with him again.'

Jack's age – he was sixty-nine at the time – was beginning to tell, though. It wasn't just London prices that shocked him: he didn't like the traffic and was clearly eager to get back home to California. Sometimes he would fret about trivial matters in the way older people do. But that didn't stop him from being extremely generous. For a start he gave me a photograph signed, 'To Keith – with my respect, my thanks and my very best wishes always. Jack Lemmon.' And then, on his last day in town, before I drove the couple back to Heathrow, Jack asked me to take them to a shop on Regent Street, where his wife wished to return a pen she had bought the previous day because it had already broken ('And such an expensive pen, too. Already broken. Really honey, maybe we should get you another one when we get back to the States.')

After Felicia scrambled out of the car, Jack asked Peter, a

representative of the film company who was with them to go with Felicia to look after her. When the two of us were left alone in the car, it turned out that he had an ulterior motive for getting everyone to leave us alone. Jack produced an envelope. 'I'd like you to have this,' he said. 'Open it later.' I did and found enclosed £200. Most of the film stars I've driven, incidentally, don't give you any tip at all; a tip of that magnitude for just a couple of days' work is almost unheard of.

Another legendary American film star, but one who is as different from Jack Lemmon as the sun is from the moon, is John Malkovich. John was born on December 9, 1953, in Benton, Illinois. He was a broody child, and his family is said to have locked him out of the family home when he became particularly difficult. One of five children, John's mother Joe Anne owned the *Benton Evening News*, while his father Dan was an environmentalist. John's career started with the famous Steppenwolf Theater Company in Chicago; thereafter he has become an international star through films such as *Dangerous Liaisons*, in which he played the scheming Vicomte De Valmont – the role that made him famous – *Empire Of The Sun* and, of course, *Being John Malkovich*, in which he stars as himself. John was married for six years to the actress Glenne Headly in the 1980s and after a brief relationship with Michelle Pfeiffer, with whom he starred in

*Dangerous Liaisons*, he is now settled with his second wife Nicoletta Peyran.

There is a brooding, intensive quality to John both on and off the screen; unlike Jack, he is not gentle and easy-going. Nor does he live amongst the film crowd; these days, he spends most of his time in France. And although he usually keeps it in check, John retains that explosive temperament he had in childhood, as I discovered when I spent a day driving him around in 1994. We had gone shopping with John's son, who was two at the time, and a woman from his film company. After we'd stopped at a few places on Sloane Street, I saw a familiar-looking car in the background.

'John,' I said, 'I'm sorry about this, but I'm afraid the paparazzi are on to us. What do you want me to do?'

His reaction was very reasonable. 'That's all right, I don't mind, don't worry,' he replied. 'I want to go to a book shop on the King's Road. Can you take me there?'

I did and, with the paparazzo still in pursuit, dropped him round the corner from the shop. John set off with his son in tow, leaving myself and the lady from his film company in the car. The two Malkoviches looked rather touching together: John, who is a huge bear of a man, walking down the street hand in hand with a little toddler, looking as if he had not a care in the world. But less than a minute later he was back, racing along the path, carrying his son and yelling his head off. He threw his son back gently in to the car, made sure he was all right, whirled round and began running towards the shop where he had been buying books. Anxious to find out what was going in, I jumped out of the car, leaving his son with the lady from his film company, and followed him.

'I said you could take pictures of me but not of my son,' John was bellowing at the top of his voice. 'Don't you people understand that they can be subject to a kidnap threat?' By this time he'd reached the photographer. He grabbed him, ripped his T-shirt and smashed the man's camera to the floor. 'I fucking warned you!' he was yelling. 'I fucking told you not to take pictures of my son!' The photographer had long black hair: John grabbed it and forced the guy's head down with his left arm and I could see him drawing his right arm back for a punch. 'I fucking warned you!' he bellowed again. Just as he was about to punch the guy, I hurled myself forward to grab his arm and pull him off. John Malkovich is very big, very heavy and very strong and it was a hell of a job to hold him back. But he'd completely lost control of himself and was screaming and shouting so much that I was really worried about what he was going to do next – in fact he was very nearly hysterical with anger and I was getting more panic-stricken by the second. If I allowed John to hit the photographer and he was prosecuted for it, there was no telling what would happen. Then again, I sympathised with him. There's a fine line in the business about getting valid pictures for public interest and intruding on someone's privacy and when the star has actually volunteered to pose for pictures if his child is left alone, then my sympathy is with the star.

At that moment – thankfully, because I wasn't going to be able to hold him for much longer – a policeman came round the corner. 'What's going on?' he asked.

'I want you to press charges!' yelled the photographer, who a second earlier had seemed as if he was about to run for his life. 'I want him to be nicked!'

The policeman took in the situation at a glance: a foaming-at-the-mouth John still yelling about the snapper trying to take pictures of his child, me hanging on for dear life and the irate photographer, done out of a very nice little fee from whatever paper would buy the pictures up. 'I'm afraid it's a civil matter,' said the policeman politely. 'If you want to press charges you'll have to do it yourself.'

'That's not good enough!' yelled the photographer. 'He assaulted me!'

'I did not assault you!' bellowed John. 'I was just stopping you from taking pictures of my son!'

The two of them started roaring at each other again (at

least John was doing no more punching and I was able to let him go) and after the policeman convinced the snapper it was better just to leave it and go away, we got back in to the car with John still fuming. 'Do you believe that?' he asked the woman from the film company. 'That guy was taking pictures of my son. I can not believe these people. I was totally prepared to let him take pictures of me but when he starts on my son, that is totally out of order. I should have punched him,' he said, looking at me in the mirror. 'He totally deserved it. I can not believe what he was trying to do.'

'John,' I said, 'I'm sorry I had to pull you off like that but just think of the consequences if you'd punched him. You'd have ended up in court and the whole situation would have got even worse. Apart from anything else, they could have taken away your passport and then you'd both have to stay here. It could have turned in to a nightmare.'

John didn't answer immediately. He went quiet, but continued to pummel the backs of the seats and muttered to the woman in the back. Then there was complete silence. John's son had fallen asleep and I saw John watching him quietly.

The silence lasted until we arrived at Pinewood. John got out of the car and, to my enormous surprise, came around and pressed a £50 note on me. 'Thank you,' he said, shaking my hand. 'You saved me from a lot of trouble. I want you to know I appreciate that.' And with that he set off, with his adoring little son safely in tow. The photographer never did press charges – John would probably have been able to plead intense provocation in any case – and I hear he has been more careful about harassing celebrities since then.

\* \* \* \* \*

Another sizeable actor – although his size is about all he has in common with John Malkovich – is Steven Segal, star of various instantly forgettable blockbusters such as *Hard to Kill, Marked for Death* and others too numerous (and insignificant) to mention. I met him only briefly but the first thing struck me was his height: when he got up from a chair, he just seemed to keep going up and up … He was also solid muscle. When I met him he was surrounded by security but Lord knows why – you'd have to be an idiot to take him on. Not only is he huge and strong, but he's a black belt in practically every martial art known to man.

I met Steven when he was in London to promote *Under Siege* in 1992, one of the few decent films he's ever made, and one that gave him the opportunity him to indulge in some highly energetic behaviour. For the first couple of days, everything was fine. I took him on a round of interviews and

222

to do some shopping and sightseeing: Steven was perfectly polite, if a little unforthcoming, and we passed a pleasant couple of days together. Then came the night of the film's premiere in Leicester Square, followed by a party at The Dorchester, where Steven was staying.

The party itself was held in a club in the basement, while I and my fellow drivers whiled away our time on the ground floor. And so it was that I was in a perfect position to see a very familiar figure, six feet-plus and bulging with muscles, escort a pretty girl up to a room in the hotel. We all raised our eyebrows and said nothing – this is not unusual behaviour for a film star. In due course Steven rejoined the party and nothing more was said. Nothing more, that is, until about half an hour later when we looked up to see Steven escorting a second pretty girl deep in to the echelons of the hotel. And after that followed a third and then a fourth ... Clearly all the martial arts training had built up some incredible reserves of stamina. Nor did this turn out to be particularly unusual behaviour for Steven – he has now been divorced three times, most recently from the beautiful film star Kelly LeBrock, who shot to fame in the mid-1980s in *Weird Science*.

While he was here, Steven was actually involved in a real-life incident that could have come straight out of one of his films. It happened as he was leaving the country in a private jet. The jet had started off down the runway and was moving quickly when Heathrow was suddenly rocked by an explosion. Two mortar bombs had been fired on to the runway. I later learned that the jet had just reached that crucial point at which to abort take-off would be lethal and so, with the airport exploding in the background, the jet continued on its way and lifted off a moment later, its passenger borne safely away from the mayhem. I would have given a good deal to know what Steven was thinking at the time.

\* \* \* \* \*

There's competition between us drivers as to who gets to drive whom and so I was miffed to learn, when Mel Gibson visited England in the early 1990s, that I would be driving not him but his wife – for some reason, the two had been designated separate limousines. The man who'd picked the plum job was German, even though he had lived in England all his life, so I decided to show him the way I felt – in the most light-hearted way possible, of course.

We were both due in Luton at 4 a.m. I made sure I was there well before him – and I put a beach towel on the chair next to mine. 'You've got to be up early to catch us

English out!' I informed him brightly when he arrived. He responded with a grunt; for some reason he wasn't very amused. Then we jumped to attention as Mel arrived. I was vaguely aware of a pair of flashing teeth walking past and that was the end of my association with Braveheart. His wife Robyn appeared to be perfectly pleasant, though.

\* \* \* \* \*

Occasionally, Hollywood greats turn out to be anything but, and it can be very disillusioning when you find out that in real life, they're actually very difficult. I always enjoyed Danny Glover's film, especially the *Lethal Weapon* series, in which he co-starred with Mel, but my brief meeting with the man himself left me with a very strong desire never to see him ever again under any circumstances. I was given a one-off job with Danny: to collect him from his London hotel at 8.30 a.m. and get him to Heathrow in time to catch the 10.30 a.m. Concorde. It couldn't have been simpler. I started reasonably enough: 'Morning Mr Glover!' I said brightly, as he and his minder appeared.

'Hmph,' he grunted and the two of them got in to the car.

I set off at some speed because this was actually quite a tight schedule and I was worried that if we hit any bad traffic we could be quite seriously delayed. Nor did I say anything – you don't, in this business, unless your passenger should want to talk to you. A moment later, however, there was an interruption from the back of the car. 'Wait, man,' he said. 'Before we get to Heathrow, I want to go to Brixton to get some Jamaican patties to take with me to eat.'

As a driver, you're in an impossible position when this happens. If I'd said yes and driven him to Brixton, we'd have missed the plane and the sky would have fallen in. If you try to be sensible, then you end up in even more trouble, and that was what happened on this occasion. 'I'm very sorry, Mr Glover,' I replied, 'but there's no time. It's an hour to Heathrow and then you've got to check in.'

'I said I want to get those patties!'

'There really, truly isn't time,' I said. 'If we go there, you'll miss your plane.' I put my foot on the accelerator and we drove on.

There was a short silence followed by an outburst as, before my very eyes, a fifty-something man looked like he turned in to a small child. 'I want those patties!' he screamed. 'I want to get them! Why were you late turning up at the hotel, we could have gone to Brixton –'

'I wasn't late,' I said. 'I was told to turn up at 8.30.'

'I want those patties! I want to go to Brixton! Someone should have told you! I WANT THOSE PATTIES!' this kind of thing can happen, of course, When you get to be a major star, you are so pampered and cosseted that you really do come to believe that the world revolves around you – well, some people do, anyway – and even when someone is trying to get you to Concorde on time, you simply see it as someone disobeying your will.

At this point, I had to draw up at a traffic light. Danny opened the door and flounced out of the car still screaming about those blinking patties. Luckily we were in Hyde Park and Danny's minder was still in the car with him: 'Wait here, I'll get him back,' he said in a resigned tone.

I waited and could see him trying to placate Danny in the distance, while snatches of 'I want those patties!' floated across the park. Eventually his minder persuaded Danny back in to the car, where I got another display of temper, this time in the guise of the silent treatment. Danny stared rigidly ahead, quivering with rage throughout the journey, absolutely dead silent and with an expression on his face that wouldn't have looked out of place on a gorgon. Finally, and not a moment too soon, we got to Heathrow. Danny flounced out of the car, slamming the door as hard as he could behind him. And they say maturity comes with age.

\* \* \* \* \*

Sometimes in this business you end up driving not the star but close members of his or her family for an extended period, and so it was that I came to spend a delightful few days in the company of Frank Sinatra's granddaughters AJ and Amanda. Frank was in London in 1990 to do some concerts and the two – Nancy's daughters, then fourteen and fifteen – had accompanied Frank and his wife Barbara for the week. I was slightly awed when I was introduced to Frank himself: he was smaller than I expected, but a very handsome man with a deep tan and those incredible blue eyes. He had a real presence: when Frank Sinatra was in the room, you knew it. He was relaxed and didn't like fuss around him – what he did like was Jack Daniel's, lots of it, after a show. His wife Barbara was a very attractive woman for her age, too. The last of Frank's four wives, Barbara had linked up with Ol' Blue Eyes after the disintegration of his marriage to Mia Farrow ('She don't talk, she don't eat – what do she do?' Frank's mother was alleged to have said of Mia) and the two were eventually married for well over twenty years. Barbara knew how to keep him happy. She didn't let herself go, she fussed over him and, along with his staff, she made sure that everything went smoothly wherever he was in the world.

The girls called him Grandpapa and clearly adored him.

They had been brought along to keep their grandparents company, as well as to see a beautiful capital city and they seemed to love every minute of it. What they were less happy about, however, was that Grandpapa insisted that they were accompanied by a minder at all times. The minder in question was the biggest man I have ever seen in my life: a veritable mountain of a man, with a Mohican haircut and ears ringed with earrings. He wore a suit, but you could tell it wasn't his usual wear. The girls liked him, but were rather intimidated by him as well. 'I'm going to have a word with Grandpapa and ask if he really has to be with us all the time,' announced Amanda. She had her word but to no avail; what Grandpapa said went and they were to stay minded. Frank was as aware as anyone of the dangers to the children and grandchildren of the rich and famous and he was clearly taking no chances.

AJ and Amanda were not to be thwarted: there was some muttering and plotting in corners while they decided what to do. Then the girls tried another ploy: they sneaked out of The Savoy, where we were all staying, and went window shopping in nearby Covent Garden. Of course, in no time at all their absence was noted and panic stations were manned: Frank was roaring at the top of his voice that we had to find them, the hotel was in turmoil and everyone was shouting their head off.

We were sent out in posses to roam the nearby streets, but it proved impossible to find them. A couple of hours later the girls turned up, blithely unaware of the pandemonium they'd caused and terribly pleased that they had got a few hours in London completely on their own. Frank was beside himself with worry, followed by anger once he'd registered they had returned safely. I was not present at the subsequent meeting with Grandpapa but I gather from those who were that the girls were told in no uncertain terms that they had to have a minder with them because of who they were and if there were any repeat episodes like that, they were going to find themselves in serious trouble. There were no further attempts to sneak out of the hotel after that.

They were lovely girls, though, and it was a pleasure to drive them around London sightseeing and shopping. You see so many jaded professionals in this business that it was a delight to be with two enthusiastic teenagers, even if they had been in the company of the rich and famous from the first moment they were born. One day they decided they wanted to go to see the Cutty Sark in Greenwich, so I arranged the trip for the following day. 'You won't be needing me,' I said. 'You get a boat from just opposite the hotel and it will take you all the way. I'll take you around again the next day.'

'No, but we want you to come,' said Amanda.

'Please come,' said AJ.

'Come with us!' they chorused in unison and so I went. The four of us – needless to say, Man Mountain was also in attendance – had a delightful day: the girls were intrigued by the Cutty Sark and loved roaming around Greenwich. When it got to lunchtime, they asked us if it would be all right to find an Italian restaurant. 'Is that okay?' asked AJ.

'Of course, whatever you want,' I said. 'You two girls are the boss.'

'Our treat!' the girls sang and so they took Man Mountain and myself out to lunch. The two were extremely knowledgeable about restaurants and Italian food and socially totally accomplished: in no time at all they were the perfect hostesses, making sure Man Mountain and myself had everything we wanted and fussing over us like two little Italian matrons in miniature. I can quite understand why Frank was so proud of them. Over lunch the conversation turned to Frank's concerts, as they'd attended one the previous night: 'It was very good,' said AJ. 'But then Grandpapa's concerts always are.'

On the day we were to leave, I was sitting in the security room at The Savoy – most hotels have these rooms, where drivers like me and all the other staff a star needs to hand can relax when we're not needed. Usually we are provided with food and drink and that was the case now. We drivers love The Savoy: it does the best steak sandwiches in London. A group of us, myself included, were getting stuck in to these when a pile of photographs was sent down to the room for us all to sort through and it turned out that this lot were pictures of Frank, for all the people who had been working with him.

Some way down the pile, one of the photographs was already in a frame. I wasn't really paying attention, assuming it must be for someone important and that I'd just get a standard signed picture of Frank, when to my enormous surprise, the framed photo was handed to me. It was a glorious picture of Frank in his prime, clad in full evening dress, and that would have been enough in itself. On the picture, however, was a message from Frank: 'For Keith – many thanks for all your help in showing the girls your marvellous city! All the best to you – Frank Sinatra.' Dumbstruck, I stared at the picture. Suddenly there was a giggle. 'We framed it!' said a voice, and there were AJ and Amanda.

Before I could say anything, AJ handed me a package. 'One day, when we're as famous as Grandpapa, we'll buy you a real one,' she said and after saying their goodbyes, the girls ran off. 'Open it later,' they cried behind them. I waited until I got home, because I wanted to have a moment to appreciate what those two lovely girls had done for me and I couldn't believe it when I finally opened my present. Inside was a foot-long model of a black Lamborghini Contache.

13

# Models Inc

IT WAS SEPTEMBER 1996 and we were all sitting around the control room of the company I worked for at the time, having a cup of tea. The mood was a mellow one. None of us much felt like working; we were all rather hoping for a long weekend. And then the call came in for a Friday job.

'Sorry mate, no can do,' said my fellow driver Dave to the Controller. 'I've booked to go away.'

'And I promised to take the missus out for a day,' said John.

'My mum's coming for tea,' said Pete.

'My daughter's in a play,' said Chris.

'I've got to take the car in for servicing,' said Derek.

'Oh shame,' said the Controller. 'The call's to drive Sam Fox.'

There was silence for a moment. Then everyone began shouting louder than everyone else – 'Well, I can always cancel my holiday,' 'The missus will understand,' 'My mum's on a diet anyway,' 'The play goes on – '

'Shut up the lot of you!' shouted the Controller. 'The job's going to Keith.'

For those of you who have been living on Planet Vulcan for the last couple of decades, Samantha Fox was *the* Page 3 girl of the 1980s. With the personality of a cockney sparrow and a body built like a shorter Brigitte Bardot, Sam was every working man's favourite pin-up. As we were all later to discover, not one of us had a chance, but no one knew that back then. All we knew was that Sam was gorgeous and we all wanted to meet her. And it turned out that I was to be the lucky man.

I walked up to her front door that day with a spring in my step and gladness in my heart. 'Hello, I'm here to pick up Sam,' I said to her manager, Chris Bonacci.

'She'll be right out,' said Chris and I returned to the car.

I saw Sam appear at the door and exchange a little banter with Chris before getting in to the car. In real life, she's even prettier than she appears in her pictures. 'Hello, I'm Sam,' she said brightly. 'Do you want a cigarette?'

'That's very kind, but I'm not allowed to.'

'I won't tell if you don't tell.'

'No, really, I prefer not to,' I said and off we went.

The first inkling I got that her manager might be more than a manager was when I realised quite how often Samantha was ringing her from the car. She was doing promotional work around London and she was extremely friendly everywhere we went, but she didn't seem to be able to stop talking to that manager. The next clue came when she rang her manager to tell her where to meet for dinner. Much as you might get on well with your employees, you don't necessarily go to restaurants with them, especially when you've been on the phone to them all day. When the manager got there, I was convinced that they were, in fact, lovers. It wasn't that either of them said anything very much; rather, it was their body language that gave things away. They kept touching one another and holding hands and the banter between them now had a definite overtone to it.

I drove Sam and her friend around for the next couple of days and she remained as friendly as ever, giving me a kiss and a cuddle when we met up and remaining her usual chirpy self. Despite the fact that she'd been a celebrity for a long time now, Sam still gave every appearance of being a teenage girl on her first trip to the West End: 'We're all going uptown,' she would cry as I drove her and her friends to a club. But as time wore on I became more and more sure that Samantha Fox, the UK's ultimate pin-up girl, was gay.

When I got back to the office a few days later, all the men were desperate to know what she was like. 'She's absolutely lovely, but she's no good for us,' I told them.

'What?' said John. 'What do you mean?'

'She's gay,' I said, flatly.

Again there was silence for a moment, and then they all started. 'Samantha Fox? Gay? You been drinking?' scoffed Dave.

'I'll bet you a tenner she's not,' said Chris.

'Yeah, I'll bet you a tenner …' came the common cry and for the next few days, they all teased me constantly about my patently ridiculous idea that Samantha Fox preferred women to men.

A few years later of course it came out that the manager was in fact Sam's girlfriend. Sam has been badly let down by the men in her life: she ended up suing her father, while she had a string of disastrous affairs with men who lied to her and cheated on her. 'Sam trusts women implicitly,' a friend once said. 'She had a lot of problems with her father, which have been well-documented. But even before that she was a "girlie girl".

'She has had many relationships with men, but she admitted to me that she felt badly let down, robbed and betrayed by them. Since then, the shutters have definitely been down as far as men are concerned.

'I do remember thinking quite clearly that she was totally anti-men in every way – emotionally, psychologically and sexually – and it wasn't just the fact that she had been wounded by her business dealings. She just had an innate mistrust of men. But with girls, Sam is very open, very girlie, very giggly. She just enjoys all that small-time girl chat. I have never seen her in a social situation "put out" to men. She does not hold her body or use her eyes in a "come on" way.'

Sam had problems with men right from the start. Her first boyfriend was Stephen Moriaty, who worked in Stroud Fruiterers in North London. Before being discovered by the *Sun*, Samantha had a Saturday job there, which is how the couple met. Stephen, unfortunately, repaid her affection with a lurid article entitled 'My Wild Sex With Sam', which detailed love-making on cartons of raspberries. It was 'all lies', according to Sam.

The cockney sparrow's next boyfriend was an unmitigated disaster. He was Peter Foster, a young Australian entrepreneur who wooed her with a red Mercedes tied up in a silk bow, followed by tickets for her parents to go to New York, where Sam was doing some work at the time. Sam adored him until she discovered he was using her name to promote a slimming drink, and was cheating on her to boot. He, too, kissed and told.

There followed a brief and disastrous fling with Kiss rocker Paul Stanley and a two-year relationship with Spanish bullfighter Rafi Camino. His family disapproved of the relationship, however, and it all ended in tears.

And Sam's relationship with her father Patrick turned as sour as her relationship with her boyfriends. Sam made an estimated £5-million fortune, but was forced to sue her father for £1.2 million of it. The two remain estranged, although her father says that he long suspected the way her life would turn out. 'I have suspected for a long time now that she has turned her back on men,' he revealed. 'It first began to dawn on me when she was living in New York some years ago. Her friends out there were all girls and were always very tearful at the airport whenever it was time for her to come back to Britain. I just wish she could have spoken to me about it, although I can understand why she didn't because it is not the easiest thing to talk about.

'But it simply not a problem for me and I want her to know that. It must be a terrible weight for Sam to carry around. I'm convinced that if she talked about it and got it all over with, she would be a lot happier. I am absolutely certain it would not hurt her career in any way. It would probably have the opposite effect. And no matter what she might think of me, or what she has been told, I have no problems with the way she lives her life.'

How very ironic, given all of this, that Sam should have become such a famous pin-up – and I wonder if it was that which made her distrust men. As a topless model, Sam received an enormous amount of attention, but it was not always the kind of attention that a woman wants. No man is perfect and confronted with naked pictures of a beautiful woman like Sam, the vast majority of men are going to judge her on appearances and nothing else. But while women enjoy being admired, if that admiration becomes too coarse it can make a woman very cynical about men. Ironic as it might seem, in some ways Sam Fox brought out the worst sides of men – and I wonder if that is the reason that she now much prefers the company of women.

Oh – and if I ever went back to collect those tenners, I'd be a rich man.

\* \* \* \* \*

Another model I met briefly was the polar opposite of Sam, both in terms of looks and personality: Naomi Campbell. I collected her from Heathrow one night in 1994 to promote her record 'Babylove', blithely unaware of her reputation for having a terrible temper, and was greeted with this vision coming out of the airport with the meet-and-greet people. 'Hello darling,' said Naomi, getting in to the back of the car and flipping open her mobile, 'drive, will you?'

I set off towards the place Naomi was staying in Hampstead, but the instructions soon changed. Naomi had spoken to a few friends and they were to meet at Browns, which necessitated a change of clothing: 'Pull up the car, darling, will you?'

I pulled up and Naomi got a change of clothing from the boot, which she proceeded to change in to in the back of the car. Afterwards she looked, if anything, even more stunning, going from jeans and a jacket to a halter top and miniskirt. I should have realised she was in the mood to party.

We got to Browns fairly late and Naomi flitted inside. I'd been told I was just taking her home, so hadn't been prepared for an all-nighter, but that was what it turned out to be. Naomi emerged from Browns at 2 a.m. and instructed me to take her to the home of the songwriter Nellie Hooper, Naomi's then boyfriend. 'I won't be long darling,' she chirped and then went inside. She emerged at 5.30 a.m. and I was eventually allowed to drive her home.

The next day I collected her at 10.30 a.m., which is the

crack of dawn in supermodel hours, and drove her from one promotional event to the next. By eight-thirty that evening, though, it was obvious that it was going to be another all-nighter, so I asked Naomi if she'd mind if I called another car in to drive her. 'Sure darling, that's fine,' she replied.

I went home and collapsed in to bed, seconds later falling in to a deep and dreamless sleep. After what seemed to be about a minute – but was in fact hours later, at 1 a.m. – the phone rang. It was the Controller. 'Keith,' he said hoarsely, 'please could you go back to look after Naomi.'

'But boss, I haven't had any sleep,' I objected.

'I know, but we've got to keep her sweet and she seemed to like you. The other driver … well, they had a row and she kicked his car door in.'

'What?'

'Yes, she's left a dent all along one side of the car. Please, Keith, go and pick her up.'

I did as I was asked and arrived to collect Naomi, wondering what on earth sort of mood she'd be in after nearly destroying my colleague's car. To my great surprise, all was sweetness and light. 'Hello darling, how are you?' beamed Naomi, for all the world as if she'd spent the evening sipping cocktails rather than destroying heavy machinery. 'Will you take me to Nellie's?'

I don't know why, but Naomi liked me. The other drivers

loathed her, given the fact that she was constantly bad tempered and abusive, but we always got on like a house on fire. I like to think it was because of my natural charm ...

# Boy Bands

M Y FIRST ENCOUNTER with a boy band was with New Kids On The Block, who were very popular in the late 1980s and early 1990s. Mob hysteria followed them everywhere they went, with girls smuggling themselves in to the hotel to meet their heroes – and, when they succeeded in getting in, doing a lot more than simply having a chat. The New Kids were not quite as clean living as their name would imply. They made out with groupies, just as countless other bands have on countless occasions before and since then, and when girls didn't make it in to the hotel, they would get their security people to smuggle them in.

New Kids On The Block consisted of Jordan Knight,

Donnie Wahlberg, Joe McIntyre, Danny Wood and Jon Knight, and they followed in the grand old tradition of manufactured bands. In 1984, following the loss of his prior discovery, New Edition, Maurice Starr decided to form a new band. Together with Mary Alford, he auditioned 500 young hopefuls for his new group, including two of Donnie's friends, Chris Hasberg and Edward Russell, but the duo didn't male the ultimate line-up as they were considered unsuitable. A third friend, Peter Fitzgerald, joined initially, but was forced to leave the band as his mother wanted him to concentrate on school. Mark Wahlberg, Donnie's brother, was also briefly a member but was never really interested in the band and quit shortly after joining.

The first recruit was Donald E Wahlberg from Dorchester, Massachusetts, a rapper, a singer and a break-dancer. He was followed by Jamie Kelley, also a rapper and a break-dancer. Jordan Nathaniel Marcel Knight was a great singer as well as a dancer and became the most famous member of the group. Daniel Wood was dedicated and self-disciplined and Jonathan Rashleigh Knight (Jordan's older brother) was an excellent singer – although bizarrely, his first love was not singing but gardening.

Initially, there were teething problems. Jamie Kelley was replaced in 1985 by twelve-year-old Joseph Mulrey

McIntyre. By 1986 the group was given the name New Kids On The Block and signed up with Columbia Records. However, their first album, called *New Kids On The Block*, failed. In their second, though, *Hangin' Tough*, they began to find some measure of success.

Their real breakthrough came in 1988 when Tiffany did her first major tour and chose New Kids On The Block as her opening act. While touring with her the New Kids enjoyed their first top ten hit with the track 'Please Don't Go Girl'. They went on to enjoy major commercial success, becoming the first teen boy band ever to achieve four top ten hits from one album in the US. Their fifth single, 'Cover Girl', also went in to the top ten.

In the UK they enjoyed seven consecutive top ten hits in 1990 and they were the first American group to achieve six consecutive top five hits in Britain. They also performed fourteen shows in Wembley Arena in 1991, which is where I came to meet them.

The boys were an odd combination of youth and maturity – screamed at by fans, cosseted by their management and yet strangely innocent in their behaviour. They would stage mock fights in the halls of the hotels in which they stayed, just as most teenagers do, and secretly smoke dope and hope their management wouldn't find out. They were decent people, too: on one occasion when I drove them in to Wembley, a surging crowd brought the barrier down. One girl was hurt and taken to hospital with a badly damaged leg; the boys were very upset by this and sent her a bunch of flowers.

But it was the attentions of the girls that really marked the New Kids out. On one occasion I took a wrong turning in the hotel and found myself in the laundry room – along with a whole pack of the prettiest laundry girls I've ever seen. They all jumped guiltily as I went in and then one of them recognised me as a New Kid employee. 'It's him!' she screamed. 'It's one of the drivers! He can get us in to the cars!' I froze as the girls all took this on board: 'Yes!' they screeched. 'Help us! Please help us get to them! We have to be with the Kids!' I was in my late thirties at the time and nothing and no one scared me, but this was something else. I turned on my heels and fled, with the girls racing behind me screaming, 'We have to get to them! We have to see the Kids! Please help us, please!'

I rounded a corner and nearly crashed in to an open door; one of the other drivers had heard what was happening and jumped out to help me. He yanked me back in to the room – it was the security room, where the drivers went to rest between jobs – slammed the door and locked it. A moment later the posse of girls turned the corner and we could hear them racing off down the corridors, yelling that they wanted to meet their heroes. 'That was a close one,' I said, mopping my brow. 'Have you got a fag, mate?'

'You shouldn't smoke,' said an unfamiliar voice – a very young, female and unfamiliar voice. 'The Kids don't smoke.' The other driver and I turned to where the voice was coming from and saw three – yes, three – adolescent girls emerging from behind one of the sofas. 'We thought we would find you here,' another of them said, as they began to move towards us. 'We bribed one of the waiters,' said the third, as I began to edge towards the door. 'We gave him twenty pounds. Now, are you going to help us?' The other driver was at the door. The girls were all looking at me, so they didn't notice him unlocking it. 'Are you going to help us?' they kept saying. 'Do you have anything that belongs to the Kids in your car? Could we have it as a souvenir? Can we drive with you? Can you get us in to meet –'

'Keith, this way!' shouted the other driver. He'd got the door open and had leapt through it, pausing only to beckon me. 'This way Keith! They can't go in to the main bit of the hotel!'

That was entirely correct – they would have been marched out in a second – so I launched myself after him and we raced up some stairs leading in to the main body of the hotel. 'Did you see the look in their eyes?' asked my new mate when we had reached safety. 'It was … terrifying.'

'Tell me about it,' I agreed. 'The female of the species is a lot deadlier than the male, especially when she's only fourteen and crazed with hormones.'

That wasn't the end of it. They tried to get in to the cars and even in to the boots, although we soon put a stop to that. But somehow they managed to keep infiltrating the hotel, which meant that whenever a maid opened a store cupboard a girl would fall out – the maids were a good deal less scared of them than we were and would turf them out in no uncertain terms – and a lot of very young girls seemed to be wandering around dressed as hotel staff. 'How do the boys deal with it?' I asked my fellow driver as we prepared to run the gamut of screaming teenagers outside and open the doors to the cars.

'They're young. They've got energy,' said my friend reasonably. After another moment, though, he shuddered. 'But rather them than me.'

\* \* \* \* \*

My next boy band – a very different lot altogether – was U2, the Irish band that was formed way back in the 1970s. I first encountered them when I went to pick up Adam Clayton, who was once engaged to my old friend Naomi Campbell. I met him at Heathrow, when he came through with his fellow band member The Edge and his girlfriend. The same old thrill, which always hit me when I met show business legends, went through me, although our encounter was brief in the extreme: 'I've been stuck in the studio for four or five weeks,' Adam commented as I drove him to his connecting flight to Spain. 'Got to clear away the cobwebs.' And that was that.

I got the chance to observe the band at slightly greater length when I drove Bono to the site of the video shoot for 'Discotheque'. It was a Friday afternoon and the shoot was taking place at Elstree. 'We're going to stay there till it's done,' said Bono as I parked the car. 'The boys won't be let out till it's all over.'

'And how long will that take?' I asked, opening the door.

'Oh, a couple of days maybe. Who knows?'

The video was actually finished on Saturday night, about thirty-six hours after they started, and the boys didn't take so much as a catnap until it was done. I did, because I was there the whole time as well, but they just got livelier and livelier as they went on. And it was an impressive video as well: it showed a huge silver sphere filled with flashing lights, which opened to reveal the band inside. I was discussing it in the green room when suddenly the door opened and one of the smallest women I have ever seen in my life came in. I thought I vaguely recognised her from somewhere, but I couldn't quite place her. 'Hey guys, how's it going?' she asked. 'Oh tea, how lovely. Do you mind if I have a cup of tea, too?'

She was not only tiny, she was extremely pretty. I jumped up to help her – as did a couple of the other men – and gave her a cup. 'So how's business?' she asked. She was definitely familiar. I thought I must have met her before. 'Pretty good, keeping busy,' I said. 'And how about you?'

'Well, you know, I haven't been doing too much stuff lately, but I'm about to bring out a new record,' she said. 'I've just spent some time with my family in Australia, which was great. I'm really looking forward to getting back in to the music scene.'

Record? Australia? Music scene? Suddenly, it clicked. I was talking to Kylie Minogue! 'This is really quite something, isn't it?' she went on, waving her hand towards where the video was being shot. 'Really impressive. I'd like to do something like this myself.' I later discovered that Kylie was going out at the time with Stephane Sednaouis, who was making the video.

By the end of the shoot, the band were still in fine spirits, with only Adam Clayton looking a bit weary. 'Champagne!' cried Bono. 'We need champagne!' Dave, the other driver, and I were dispatched to go and get two crates of champagne: on our return we started acting as waiters and serving it out to everyone. 'Okay boys, we're all to hit the town tonight!' cried Bono and there was much roaring of approval – although in the end, much to my disappointment, everyone went home.

I was driving Bono and The Edge and to hear the two of them talking, half the time you would never have guessed they were major international rock stars. There was some chat about music, the video and the tour but on the whole it was more about family – Bono, especially, is a great family man and very down to earth with it.

\* \* \* \* \*

The same can be said for another great rock star whom I was privileged to meet: Bruce Springsteen. I drove him around the day after he did a concert at Wembley: he was pleased that the gig had gone well while his wife, Patty Scialfa, was taking full advantage of the shopping facilities in London. 'I thought more about what we should be doing for our home, honey,' she said as I drove them to lunch at the Bombay Brasserie. 'There are some great stores in London and I got some great new ideas ...'

'Just do it, honey,' said The Boss, patting her knee.

When the couple came out of the Bombay Brasserie, I opened the door of the car but just as they were about to get in, we heard music coming from The Puss in Boots, the pub next door. 'C'mon, honey, let's go get a drink,' Bruce said to Patty. 'C'mon Keith, you come too.' And so I followed them as they made their way in to the pub.

The place was absolutely packed and at first, as Bruce shouldered his way to the bar to get a drink, no one really noticed his presence. But gradually word started to filter out that a Very Famous Man was in the pub on a Saturday lunchtime, just like the rest of them. People started doing double takes, but no one said anything – they were clearly wanting to ask if it was really him, but didn't want to make an idiot of themselves. Finally, someone did the obvious thing – and put a Springsteen record on the jukebox. Bruce chuckled and raised his pint of beer to the crowd.

The pub's manager materialised in front of him. 'Bruce Springsteen?' he gasped. 'Mr Springsteen? Is it really you?'

'It's me all right,' said Bruce, beaming at him. 'Say, you got a microphone around here?'

They did indeed, from karaoke nights, and it was duly found and produced. Bruce stepped on to a table. 'Okay you guys: let's rock!' he roared and began singing in accompaniment to himself on the jukebox. The crowd went absolutely wild and were singing along with him: the whole thing went on for about half an hour at the end of which Bruce insisted on leaving, although the whole place was begging him to stay. He had made the residents of that part of London very happy, though; the previous night he had been wowing the thousands at Wembley and now today he was playing for a couple of hundred people in a pub. I suspect he made quite a few fans that day.

\* \* \* \* \*

I also spent a bit of time with Status Quo, especially Francis Rossi and Rick Parfitt. Francis is a character. The first thing he'll do when he gets in to the car off an airplane is roll a joint and the second thing he'll do is to get me to stop off at a Burger King. He absolutely loves double king size chicken burger and chips. If he actually goes in, he gets recognised, so he tends to prefer drive-in places. He's very relaxed about it all.

Francis is a real family man. He's now married to his second wife Eileen and has eight children, all of whom at one time were living at his house. He has a very grand place in Surrey, with lots of marble and a swimming pool and when you turned in to his drive, you saw about thirty cars – vans, Ford Cortinas, that sort of thing – littering up the place because his boys would be there and have their friends round.

In recent years, Francis's family has come to mean much

more to him than anything else. When he was going on tour, he'd stand by the car and say, 'Keith, think of an excuse.'

'Think of an excuse for what, mate?'

'For an excuse for me not to get in to the car! I want to stay at home!' But of course, he'd always come out of it and go on tour. Unbelievably, Status Quo has been going since the early 1960s (when they all had short hair and wore ties) and none of them are going to back out now.

Rick Parfitt is also something of a character. With him it's drink rather than joints. He has a boat near where lives in Twickenham and for him, heaven is sitting on his boat, having a drink and watching the rest of the world go by. He was once known as one of the 'wild men of rock', but these days, he himself insists he's more like the 'mild man of rock'. His capacity for alcohol matches that of Keith Richards. Many's the time I've collected him late at night from his boat, only to take him to one of the local clubs, where he'll stay until morning.

I've also driven Neil Warnock – not, perhaps, a famous name in itself, but a very famous agent in the world of rock music, numbering Status Quo and Pink Floyd amongst his clients. He lives quite near Rod Stewart and one day I drove him and his wife to Alexandra Palace in London for some pop music awards. When we set off it was a glorious evening, so Neil wore just a dinner jacket and his wife an evening gown, but by the time the awards ceremony was over in the early hours of the next morning, it was snowing.

I drove the two of them back to Essex, but when we got there, we found the road too blocked up to drive up to the house. I offered to go to the house myself and get their jeep, which would have been able to get through the snow, but the two of them refused and decided to walk. And so I watched them set off for a mile-long walk in the snow, dressed for a summer day. And I never heard the end of that – 'Oh you know Keith,' Neil would always say when we met up. 'The driver who always makes you walk the last mile …'

# Finale

I T'S MANY YEARS now since I started being a chauffeur and it's time to move on. I went in to the business in the late 1980s and I've had a great time, meeting so many famous and interesting people and seeing so much of the world. But it has taken up a huge chunk of my life and now it's time to and reclaim my life as my own. My wife Jane and I are moving to the country and from now on the closest we'll get to all these famous stars is when we pick up a newspaper or turn on the television. And I'm looking forward to it: touring and performing may be exhausting for the star, but it's exhausting for all their back-up people, too. Instead of acting as bodyguard and driver, I'm looking forward to putting my feet up and doing some gardening. It's time for the next generation to come forward.

But I don't regret a minute of it, and it's brought me a lot in my personal life, too. In 1997 I was at a very low edge and, driving U2 on tour, I was beginning to wonder if it was all worth it. I had just broken up with my girlfriend of ten years' standing and living with my sister – not an ideal set-up for a grown man. Mooching around The Savoy one night, waiting for the band, I saw a very attractive redhead called Jane Garton whom I vaguely recognised from the office. It turned out that she was co-ordinating transport for the tour and so we sat down together and had a cup of coffee.

A couple of days later, backstage at Leeds in Round Hay Park, I saw Jane again. This time we started chatting properly and after the show we went out together for a late dinner. Something clicked. I found myself opening my heart to her about my failed relationship and discovered she was in exactly the same situation.

We got on better and better and I began to wonder if she could be the woman who could make me happy once again. Nothing happened at the time, though. The next day we all drove back, me in one car and Jane in another, with another man from her office. When we all stopped at a service station, her colleague eyed us both narrowly. 'I think Jane would rather be in your car, mate,' he said and so it was that we continued our journey together.

Still nothing happened, though, until a couple of days later. We had discussed going on holiday, but nothing had come of it. I then had to go and spend a day with my ex to sort out joint affairs. After a truly dreadful time I came back to find a message from Jane. 'Do you fancy taking me out to dinner tonight?' she asked. Yes I very much did, so we went off to Brighton and had dinner together by the sea. Soon afterwards we were living together and that, my friends, was that.

Jane brought a breath of fresh air in to my life and allowed me to regain the confidence I'd lost. More than that, we built up a business together. Jane had a 1990 Jaguar. To that we added (over time) a people carrier and a Mercedes. I continued to drive Mick and many of my other clients and so my happiness with Jane has been doubled: it's been both personal and professional.

All my old clients have moved on, too. Their careers have gone up, down and sideways, their personal lives have been tumultuous, fraught and sometimes even happy. Some of my old clients are no longer with us and have ascended to that great big arena in the sky. Here's a round-up of where they are now, and to them I say, thank you for the good times. There were many of them – and they sure outweighed the bad.

KEITH RICHARDS remains happily married to Patti and spends much of his time in their home in Connecticut. In 2002 he had to take a medical in preparation for the Stones' tour – their fortieth anniversary tour – and the most abused body in the history of rock 'n' roll was pronounced as fit as that of a young boy. Rumours continue to abound about feuds with Mick Jagger, especially because the latter has embarked on a number of solo projects. In fact, the two of them get on as well as they ever have done.

RONNIE WOOD  was admitted to a clinic for treatment for alcoholism in 2002, where he was given support from his old friend and fellow band member Rod Stewart. Encouraged by his concerned family and the rest of the Stones he is reported to be anxious to get his drinking under control before what will almost certainly be the last Stones tour in 2002.

CHARLIE WATTS remains the Stone who was born to be mild. Now – unbelievably – in his sixties, he continues in his day job as drummer with the Stones, while the rest of the time he plays with The Charlie Watts Quintet. He and Shirley continue to run their stud farm in Devon.

JERRY HALL has found happiness with banker Tim Attias. Speculation is rife that the couple will wed. After her London appearances in *The Graduate* and *The Vagina Monologues*, it looks as if her long-held ambition to be a serious actress may at last be coming to fruition.

MICHAEL JACKSON has been married twice in the last decade, first to Lisa Marie Presley, the daughter of Elvis, in 1994, and then to former nurse Debbie Rowe, in 1996. Both marriages ended in divorce. He and his children, Prince Michael Jackson Jnr, born in 1997 and Paris Michael Katherine Jackson, born in 1998, live on his Neverland estate in California.

ROD STEWART is happily dating leggy blonde photographer Penny Lancaster. The two actually met on the night Rod and Rachel split up. Rachel has had a couple of brief romances and is now dating the singer Robbie Williams.

BILL WYMAN, Suzanne and their three daughters live happily in Chelsea, Suffolk and the South of France. Bill has started to write about architectural history in Suffolk and continues to tour with The Rhythm Kings.

BARBRA STREISAND is now married to the actor James

Brolin. James's son Josh was engaged to the British actress Minnie Driver, but Minnie called off the wedding amidst rumours that her future step-mother-in-law was interfering too much.

JULIA ROBERTS has had dizzying success with her career, winning the Oscar for Best Actress in 2001 for the title role in the film *Erin Brockovich*. Her personal life has not run so smoothly, however. Since her divorce from Lyle Lovett, she has had a series of relationships, including four years with the actor Benjamin Blatt, but has yet to settle down with anyone.

SAM FOX split up with her long-term partner Chris Bonacci in 1999 and she is now happily ensconced with her manager, Myra Stratton. Men would appear to be out of the picture for good. She once said, 'All my life it's been the same with men. Being a woman who is famous and adored by men is very hard for any boyfriend to handle. All my boyfriends end up insecure.' Sadly, her father Pat died in 2000, before the two could be reconciled.

NAOMI CAMPBELL remains the most successful black supermodel of her generation. However, her reputation has suffered in recent years amongst allegations of drug abuse and temper tantrums. She recently won a privacy case against the *Mirror*, which revealed she attended Narcotics Anonymous meetings, but was awarded the very minor sum of £3,500. Having split up with her boyfriend of some years' standing, the Italian millionaire Flavio Briattori, she too has yet to settle down.

MARIAH CAREY has had a difficult time in recent years. Now divorced from Tommy Mottola, she has had a series of breakdowns and in 2002 was dropped by her record company, EMI, with a reported settlement of £35 million. However, a new deal is in the offing and her career looks set to reignite.

GLORIA ESTEFAN remains happily married to Emilio Estefan, whom she wed when she was just twenty-one. The couple have two children, Nayib and Emily Marie, and in 2001 Gloria remarked, 'Maybe I should quit recording in English.' I fervently hope she does no such thing.

CELINE DION shot to fame in 1991 through singing the title theme of *Beauty and The Beast* with Peabo Bryson. The youngest of fourteen children, she was born in 1968 in Charlemagne, Canada and in 1994 married Rene, her long-term manager. In 2001, Celine and Rene had a son, Rene-

Charles. She has won innumerable awards since then, and her rendition of 'My Heart Will Go On' for the film *Titanic* won an Oscar for best film in 1998. In 2000, Celine and Rene renewed their wedding vows after it was discovered that Rene was suffering from skin cancer; Celine took a two-year break from her career to look after him. Her 2002 album, *A New Day Has Come*, the first for five years, went to number one in the charts.

MADONNA is now married to the British film director Guy Ritchie, who is ten years her junior. The couple live in London with her daughter Lourdes and their son Rocco and at the time of writing there is speculation that Madonna might be pregnant with her third child. The book *Sex* turned out to be a low point in her career, but Madonna wisely took some time out of the limelight and came back to re-establish herself as a serious artist. She is also establishing herself as a country woman – there has been some amusement about the fact that she is learning to shoot. And her mother-in-law, Shireen Ritchie, is a prominent member of the Conservative Party.

CHRISTOPHER CICCONE remains close to his sister. He has designed some of the most fashionable restaurants in Hollywood but he, too, is said to be still looking for love. It was reported in 1998 that Madonna tried to set him up with Rupert Everett, her co star in *The Next Best Thing*, but nothing came of it. Most recently, he has been spotted acting as Gwynneth Paltrow's walker.

REBECCA DE MORNAY has had some upheaval in her private life. Before I met her she had a brief relationship with Harry Dean Stanton (she clearly likes older men) and then lived with Ton Cruise for two and a half years after meeting him in 1983 on the set of *Risky Business*. She was then briefly married to novelist and screenwriter Bruce Wagner after which came Leonard Cohen. She is now with Patrick O'Neal, the son of Ryan O'Neal and Leigh Taylor-Young; the couple have been together since 1995. Rebecca has never quite recreated the success she had in *The Hand That Rocks The Cradle*, but continues to work regularly. At the time of writing, her most recent film, in 2001, was *A Girl Thing*.

KATE WINSLET has recovered from the trauma of her split with Jim Threapleton and is now happily ensconced with the director Sam Mendes, the director of *American Beauty*.

SAFFRON BURROWS has also split from her long-term partner, Mike Figgis, the director of *Leaving Las Vegas*. She is now said to be close friends with the actress Fiona Shaw, who plays Aunt Petunia in *Harry Potter and the Philosopher's Stone*.

JACK LEMMON and WALTER MATTHAU have both gone to that great screening room in the sky, Jack in 2001 at the age of seventy-six and Walter a year earlier, aged seventy-nine. Both remain greatly loved and sadly missed.

JOHN MALKOVICH remains one of the most respected actors of his generation. He is now based in France, where he lives with his wife Nicoletta Peyran, an Asian culture scholar he met while filming *The Sheltering Sky* in 1990 and their two children Amandine and Lowey. In 2002 John made his debut as a director with *The Dancer Upstairs*. In 1999, he appeared in the film *Being John Malkovich*, that spectacularly quirky offering about a puppeteer who finds a passage in to John Malkovich's head.

FRANCIS ALBERT SINATRA, the last of the original Rat Pack, 'bought the big casino' as he and his friends used to put it, when he died in 1998, aged eighty-two.

New Kids On The Block split up in 1994.

BRUCE SPRINGSTEEN is still The Boss.

U2 go on from strength to strength, receiving acclaim from all sides. They were awarded at the Brit Awards 2001 for their outstanding contribution to music and by early 2002 added a further four Grammy awards to an already extensive collection. Bono, in particular, has been in the news with his widely publicised support for the cancellation of third world debt.

STATUS QUO, in their own words, are 'Always rockin' somewhere!' They will be doing yet another tour in Britain and Europe towards autumn 2002.

MICK JAGGER still seems to me to be crazy about Jerry Hall.